Reading Engagement
Grade 8

By
JANET P. SITTER, Ph.D.

COPYRIGHT © 2005 Mark Twain Media, Inc.

ISBN 1-58037-292-9

Printing No. CD-404019

Mark Twain Media, Inc., Publishers
Distributed by Carson-Dellosa Publishing Company, Inc.

The purchase of this book entitles the buyer to reproduce the student pages for classroom use only. Other permissions may be obtained by writing Mark Twain Media, Inc., Publishers.

All rights reserved. Printed in the United States of America.

Table of Contents

Introduction 1
How to Use This Book 2
Reading Level Analysis for Reading Selections 4

Level One
- Lesson 1: The Scream Machine 6
- Lesson 2: Time After Time 14
- Lesson 3: Did You Know …? 24

Level Two
- Lesson 1: NASCAR 32
- Lesson 2: Titanic of the Sky 41
- Lesson 3: Lord Stanley's Cup 49

Level Three
- Lesson 1: American Royalty, Part I 56
- Lesson 2: The Day the Music Died 64
- Lesson 3: "Mr. Television" 74
- Lesson 4: Happy New Year! 82

Level Four
- Lesson 1: American Royalty, Part II 92
- Lesson 2: The United States Constitution 101
- Lesson 3: Presidential Scandals 110

Answer Keys 119

Reading Engagement: Grade 8 — Introduction

Introduction

The goal of *Reading Engagement: Grade 8* is to help students improve their reading comprehension skills. The reading selections and reading guides in this book have been developed to provide instructional reading practice for below-average and/or reluctant readers, to provide independent reading activities for the average reader, and to provide supplemental reading for the more competent readers in your classroom. By completing the readings and activities in *Reading Engagement: Grade 8,* your students will receive instruction, practice, and/or reinforcement in these strategies routinely practiced by good readers:

1. Good readers see reading as a comprehension process, not a decoding process.
2. Good readers relate what they are reading to what they already know.
3. Good readers decode rapidly, applying a number of word analysis skills to figure out unknown words.
4. Good readers know and recognize more words and have larger vocabularies.
5. Good readers monitor their comprehension and take action when they don't understand what they are reading.

Reading Engagement: Grade 8 uses interesting text to focus students' motivation and interest on what they are reading. The activities in the reading guides help students make connections between what they are reading and what they already know. The vocabulary exercises help students not only build vocabulary but learn new words in meaningful ways. The comprehension questions seek to improve the thinking skills of students by asking questions at the literal, interpretive, and applied levels of critical thinking. The reading guides provide support for comprehension before reading, during reading, and after reading. The student's comprehension is tested through a simple, informal reading assessment following each reading. And finally, each lesson contains activities to extend the student's understanding after reading.

Each lesson is designed for independent student use, though with reluctant or below-average readers, instruction might be necessary. Each lesson is independent of all the other lessons and increases in difficulty as the student moves through them. Each lesson can be treated as a unit of instruction and can become part of the student's reading portfolio.

The more students read, the better readers they become. These readings are designed to help them become better readers.

How to Use This Book

The reading lessons in this book are divided into four levels. Each level increases the difficulty of the reading, beginning with Level One, Lesson 1 at a sixth-grade reading level and continuing with incremental jumps in reading difficulty, culminating in Level Four, Lesson 3 at a ninth-grade reading level.

Level One	Level Two	Level Three	Level Four
Lesson 1 6.1	Lesson 1 7.0	Lesson 1 8.0	Lesson 1 8.9
Lesson 2 6.3	Lesson 2 7.4	Lesson 2 8.2	Lesson 2 9.0
Lesson 3 6.7	Lesson 3 7.5	Lesson 3 8.2	Lesson 3 9.0
		Lesson 4 8.6	

Each lesson contains a short 400–1,100 word story with a reading guide. The instructional framework for the Reading Guides consists of activities to do before reading the selection, during the reading of the selection, and after reading the selection.

BEFORE READING

The activities in the Before Reading section of the Reading Guides are intended to prepare the reader for the reading by:

- a. establishing a purpose for reading;
- b. building and activating background knowledge;
- c. connecting what is known to what is to be learned;
- d. presenting key concepts and vocabulary; and
- e. activating student interest and motivation.

DURING READING

The activities in the During Reading section of the Reading Guides are intended to support the reader during the reading by:

- a. encouraging readers to read actively;
- b. guiding interactions between readers and text;
- c. using questions to activate critical thinking; and
- d. checking and expanding student comprehension skills.

How to Use This Book (cont.)

AFTER READING

The activities in the After Reading section of the Reading Guides are intended to assess and extend the reader's comprehension by:

a. promoting thoughtful consideration of the text;
d. supporting the reader's comprehension with Internet experiences;
b. checking and evaluating the reader's comprehension; and
c. extending the reader's understanding of the text.

Reading comprehension skills refer to a wide range of skills readers use to get meaning from text. While these skills develop over time, the lessons in *Reading Engagement: Grade 8* provide instruction, practice, and reinforcement in the following skills.

- Identifying details
- Stating main idea
- Inferring main idea
- Recalling details
- Inferring details
- Inferring cause and effect
- Following directions
- Determining sequence
- Locating reference
- Recalling information
- Summarizing ideas
- Identifying time sequence
- Retelling in own words
- Inferring author's purpose/intent

- Comparing and contrasting
- Drawing conclusions
- Making generalizations
- Recognizing structure and organization of text
- Predicting outcomes
- Evaluating text
- Judging author's qualifications
- Distinguishing facts from opinions
- Recognizing figurative language
- Identifying mood
- Understanding mental imagery
- Recognizing signal words
- Recognizing elements of story

Reading Engagement: Grade 8

Reading Level Analysis for Reading Selections

Sample Begins: The Scream Machine
Sample Ends: to keep your arms inside!
Words: 930
Syllables: 1,406
Monosyllabic Words: 607
Words of 3 or more Syllables: 113
Sentences: 52
Syllables/Word: 1.52
Syllables/100 Words: 151.19
Monosyllabic Words/100 Words: 65.27
Polysyllabic Words/100 Words: 12.16
Sentences/100 Words: 5.60
Words/Sentence: 17.89
Reading Grade Level: 6.1

Sample Begins: Time After Time
Sample Ends: calendar begins 1 January.
Words: 914
Syllables: 1,458
Monosyllabic Words: 585
Words of 3 or more Syllables 172
Sentences: 58
Syllables/Word: 1.60
Syllables/100 Words: 159.52
Monosyllabic Words/100 Words: 64.01
Polysyllabic Words/100 Words: 18.82
Sentences/100 Words: 6.35
Words/Sentence: 15.76
Reading Grade Level: 6.3

Sample Begins: Did You Know …?
Sample Ends: and Cigar Stubbs.
Words: 602
Difficult Words (Dale-Chall): 92
Sentences: 49
Sentences/100 Words: 8.14
Words/Sentence: 12.29
% of Words Not on the Dale-Chall List: 15.29
Reading Grade Level: 6.7

Sample Begins: NASCAR
Sample Ends: roll-over in the race.
Words: 1,041
Difficult Words (Dale-Chall): 185
Sentences: 79
Sentences/100 Words: 7.59
Words/Sentence: 13.18
% of Words Not on the Dale-Chall List: 17.07
Reading Grade Level: 7.0

Sample Begins: Titanic of the Sky
Sample Ends: man's worst catastrophic catastrophes.
Words: 844
Difficult Words (Dale-Chall): 159
Sentences: 52
Sentences/100 Words: 6.17
Words/Sentence: 16.24
% of Words Not on the Dale-Chall List: 18.84
Reading Grade Level: 7.4

Sample Begins: Lord Stanley's Cup
Sample Ends: Cup is a trophy of the people.
Words: 1,065
Difficult Words (Dale-Chall): 198
Sentences: 57
Sentences/100 Words: 5.36
Words/Sentence: 18.69
% of Words Not on the Dale-Chall List: 18.60
Reading Grade Level: 7.5

Sample Begins: American Royalty, Part I
Sample Ends: Hawaii's kings were elected.
Words: 765
Difficult Words (Dale-Chall): 176
Sentences: 56
Sentences/100 Words: 7.25
Words/Sentence: 13.81
% of Words Not on the Dale-Chall List: 23.19
Reading Grade Level: 8.0

Sample Begins: The Day the Music Died
Sample Ends: rock 'n roll is played."
Words: 1,103
Difficult Words (Dale-Chall): 267
Sentences: 72
Sentences/100 Words: 6.53
Words/Sentence: 15.32
% of Words Not on the Dale-Chall List: 24.21
Reading Grade Level: 8.2

Sample Begins: "Mr. Television"
Sample Ends: but a has was once an are."
Words: 872
Difficult Words (Dale-Chall): 204
Sentences: 50
Sentences/100 Words: 5.74
Words/Sentence: 17.45
% of Words Not on the Dale-Chall List: 23.40
Reading Grade Level: 8.2

Sample Begins: Happy New Year!
Sample Ends: family, and festivities.
Words: 1,034
Syllables: 1,502
Monosyllabic Words: 736
Words of 3 or more Syllables 126
Sentences: 57
Syllables/Word: 1.46
Syllables/100 Words: 145.27
Monosyllabic Words/100 Words: 71.18
Polysyllabic Words/100 Words: 12.19
Sentences/100 Words: 5.52
Words/Sentence: 18.15
Reading Grade Level: 8.6

© Mark Twain Media, Inc., Publishers

Reading Level Analysis for Reading Selections (cont.)

Sample Begins: American Royalty, Part II
Sample Ends: "Aloha a hui hou."
Words: 441
Difficult Words (Dale-Chall): 126
Sentences: 30
Sentences/100 Words: 6.81
Words/Sentence: 14.71
% of Words Not on the Dale-Chall List: 28.58
Reading Grade Level: 8.9

Sample Begins: The United States Constitution
Sample Ends: in their beliefs, thoughts, and emotions.
Words: 870
Difficult Words (Dale-Chall): 250
Sentences: 55
Sentences/100 Words: 6.33
Words/Sentence: 15.82
% of Words Not on the Dale-Chall List: 28.74
Reading Grade Level: 9.0

Sample Begins: Presidential Scandals
Sample Ends: synonym for public corruption.
Words: 1,022
Difficult Words (Dale-Chall): 300
Sentences: 74
Sentences/100 Words: 7.25
Words/Sentence: 13.82
% of Words Not on the Dale-Chall List: 29.36
Reading Grade Level: 9.0

Reading Engagement: Grade 8   Level One, Lesson 1: The Scream Machine

Name: _____ Date: _____

Level One, Lesson 1: The Scream Machine

The Scream Machine

Are you one of the millions of people who visit amusement parks for one, and only one, reason—to ride the roller coaster? Thrill-seekers search for more death-defying thrills in their scream machines; they want more looping, higher and steeper hills, greater drops and rolls, and faster speeds. Today, the Top Thrill Dragster at Cedar Point in Sandusky, Ohio, holds the world record for largest drop (400 feet), tallest point of the track to the ground below (420 feet), and fastest (120 mph) coaster.

Roller coasters operate on a few simple laws of physics: potential and kinetic energy, gravitational pull, centrifugal force, and friction. The train of cars on the coaster is pulled slowly to the top of the first hill by a cable, collecting potential energy into the system. At the top of the first hill, the potential energy is converted to kinetic energy as the train drops down and speeds along the tracks. Different types of wheels are used to make the ride smooth, and compressed airbrakes stop the car when the ride ends. The best coasters begin with a huge drop so the train can build up enough energy for the entire ride.

Scream machines began in Russia in the 1800s. During the cold Russian winters, manmade ice-covered hills were constructed of cut lumber and tree trunks. Riders walked up 70 feet (5 stories) of stairs, climbed into ice-block sleds, and sat on straw seats. In a few seconds, the sleds roared down the hill at speeds of up to 50 mph.

The potential for profit motivated the move of the Russian Mountains (Les Montagnes Russes) to Paris in 1804. While small wheels were added to the sled for a smoother ride, little attention was paid to safety measures. In fact, the more injuries that were suffered, the greater the attendance at the ride. Thirteen years later, the Bellville Mountains and the Aerial Walks in Paris improved the original ride by adding locking wheels, continuous tracks, and cables that hoisted the cars to the top of the hill.

The first American roller coaster was built at Coney Island in New York. Coney Island was an amusement park built in 1875 at the end of the railway line. In 1884, the first 600-foot gravity switchback train was introduced. With a top speed of six miles per hour, the coaster resembled the Gravity Road roller coaster in Pennsylvania in that a ratchet rail was added to run between the two-rail tracks. This was an important addition because it prevented the cars from rolling backward. Charles Alcoke connected the ends of the track in one continuous loop in order to return riders to the station. Phillip Hinkle designed an elliptical coaster with a power hoist that pulled cars to the top of the first hill. This addition made the ride more exciting than the slow-moving Switchback.

© Mark Twain Media, Inc., Publishers

Level One, Lesson 1: The Scream Machine (cont.)

Improvements upon improvements were quickly made (and sometimes quickly eliminated) on the Coney Island Scream Machines. In 1895, Lina Beecher installed the Flip-Flap Railway at Coney Island, which had the first uncomfortable and dangerous circular loop. This 25-foot loop proved to be very popular as it whipped its riders into a frenzy. In 1901, the Loop-the-Loop was installed at Coney Island. In an attempt to minimize the gravitational pull, the coaster had a softer, oval-shaped design. The Loop-the-Loop was the pinnacle of coasters for the next five or six years until the first high-speed roller coaster, Drop-the-Dip, was introduced. With the increased speed came real concerns for safety; the Drop-the-Dip introduced lap bars, which kept passengers from rocketing out of their seats.

More than 1,500 roller coasters were in operation in the United States in the 1920s. Designers continued to push the envelope of coaster design, which encouraged greater attention to safety measures. In fact, at the famous "triplets of terror" built by Harry Traver, the Cyclone at Crystal Beach in Ontario, Lightning at Revere Beach in Massachusetts, and the Cyclone at Palisades Park in New Jersey, a nurse was always on duty on the loading platform! These three scream machines featured a 90-foot drop and hairpin turns. They were predicated on both The Fireball and The Bobs. The Fireball was the fastest coaster ever built and the first with a man-made drop. The Bobs, designed by Frederick Church and Harry Traver, had 3,253 feet of track, 16 hills, and 12 curves.

Following the Great Depression in the United States—a very slow period in coaster design—roller coasters were reborn. Walt Disney commissioned the Arrow Development Company in 1959 to design the bobsled-style Matterhorn, the first steel roller coaster. The engineers used tubular steel rails and nylon wheels, which made the rides longer and smoother. With the success of Disneyland, theme parks proliferated across America. At the very heart of these parks was the roller coaster. The first flume ride (a water ride) was introduced at Six Flags Over Texas in 1966. The helix-shaped corkscrew coaster opened at Knott's Berry Farm in California, and in 1975, the first 360-degree rolls were added to its coaster. The Great American Revolution at Six Flags Magic Mountain successfully included the first vertical loop.

The drive for the fastest, biggest, craziest coaster continues. Today some of the wildest coasters are the 60-degree, 205-foot drop of the Magnum XL-200 at Cedar Point, the 70-mile-per-hour Batman and Robin at Six Flags Great Adventure in New Jersey, and the three-minute-long, stand-up Riddler's Revenge at Six Flags Magic Mountain. The 900 coasters in operation today are a very long way from the Russian Mountains of the past. Whatever coasters of the future might be like, it will still be important to keep your arms inside!

Reading Engagement: Grade 8 Level One, Lesson 1: The Scream Machine

Name: _____ Date: _____

Level One, Lesson 1: The Scream Machine (cont.)

Reading Guide for "The Scream Machine"

BEFORE READING

Before reading "The Scream Machine," complete the **Before Reading** section of the Reading Guide.

A. Prereading Activity: Connecting Background Knowledge

Building a Scream Machine

Directions: Go to http://media.kids.discovery.com/games/rollercoasters/buildacoaster.html and build yourself a roller coaster. Print out your coaster when you are finished, and attach it to this Reading Guide.

B. Vocabulary: Science Concepts

Roller Coaster Words

Directions: Look up definitions for the words below in the glossary of your science textbook, a dictionary, or other resource. Write the definitions in the space below.

1. potential energy _____
   _____

2. kinetic energy _____
   _____

3. gravitational pull _____
   _____

4. centrifugal force _____
   _____

5. friction _____
   _____

© Mark Twain Media, Inc., Publishers

Reading Engagement: Grade 8 — Level One, Lesson 1: The Scream Machine

Name: _____ Date: _____

Level One, Lesson 1: The Scream Machine (cont.)

C. Prereading Questions

1. What do you think this reading is going to be about?

   rollercoasters

2. Read the questions in the **After Reading** section of this Reading Guide.

   a. Which question do you find the most interesting?

   _C_

   b. Which answer do you think will be hardest to find?

   _D_

3. What is your purpose for reading this story? Finish this sentence: I am reading to find out ...

   about raler coasters

DURING READING

1. Put a check mark in the margin next to the information that answers the questions in the **After Reading** section.

2. Circle any words you don't know when you come to them in the passage.

3. Put a question mark in the margin for anything you don't understand.

© Mark Twain Media, Inc., Publishers

Reading Engagement: Grade 8　　　　　　　　Level One, Lesson 1: The Scream Machine

Name: _____ Date: _____

Level One, Lesson 1: The Scream Machine (cont.)

AFTER READING

1. READING THE LINES: Answer these questions by using information in the selection.

    a. Are you the kind of person who goes to the amusement park just to ride the roller coaster? Why or why not?

    No

    b. What are the names of amusement park coasters mentioned in this reading?

    Dragster

    c. How did roller coasters begin?

    People use to go Down Ice Hills

    d. Why was the ratchet rail an important addition to coasters?

    It Direged

© Mark Twain Media, Inc., Publishers　　　10

Reading Engagement: Grade 8   Level One, Lesson 1: The Scream Machine

Name: _____ Date: _____

Level One, Lesson 1: The Scream Machine (cont.)

2. READING BETWEEN THE LINES: Answer these questions by inferring ideas in the selection.

   a.   What is the main idea of this reading?

_____

_____

_____

_____

   b.   What does "potential for profit" in the first sentence of paragraph four mean?

_____

_____

_____

   c.   In paragraph four, sentence three, it says, "... the more injuries that were suffered, the greater the attendance at the ride." Why?

_____

_____

_____

_____

   d.   In paragraph six, sentence six says, "The Loop-the-Loop was the pinnacle of coasters ..." What does this mean?

_____

_____

_____

_____

© Mark Twain Media, Inc., Publishers

Level One, Lesson 1: The Scream Machine (cont.)

3. **READING BEYOND THE LINES:** Answer these questions with your own opinions.

   a. Have you ever ridden a really scary roller coaster? What was it like?

   _____

   _____

   _____

   _____

   b. Why do you think some people are thrill seekers and some are not?

   _____

   _____

   _____

   _____

   c. What safety measures do modern coasters have? Are they enough? Why or why not?

   _____

   _____

   _____

   _____

ASSESSMENT/REINFORCEMENT

A. To really understand how a roller coaster works, go to www.search.eb.com/coasters/ride.html.

Level One, Lesson 1: The Scream Machine (cont.)

B. Put each word about roller coasters in the corresponding category.

ALL ABOUT ROLLER COASTERS

WORD BANK

barrel roll	The Beast	The Big One	bobsled	brakes
cars	chains	circuit	corkscrew	Cyclone
helix	hills	hypercoaster	inversion	inverted
lap bars	looping	loop-the-loop	Matterhorn	motors
out-and-back	portable	rails	seats	shuttle
Son of Beast	suspended	tracks	twister	Volcano

PARTS/FEATURES

_____
_____
_____
_____
_____
_____
_____
_____

TYPES OF ROLLER COASTERS

_____
_____
_____
_____
_____
_____
_____
_____

FORMATIONS

_____
_____
_____
_____

NAMES OF ROLLER COASTERS

_____
_____
_____
_____

Level One, Lesson 2: Time After Time

Time After Time

Over the millennia, many different calendars have been developed to help people organize their lives. In fact, there are about forty different calendars used in the world today, mostly to determine religious dates. Most modern countries use the Gregorian (or Christian) calendar for official civic activities. Calendars are most commonly based on astronomical events, particularly the motion of the earth around the sun and the moon around the earth.

The Christian Calendar

The Christian Calendar, also known as the Gregorian calendar, serves as an international standard for civil use, and it regulates the ceremonial cycle of the Roman Catholic and Protestant churches (which was its original purpose). The order of the months and the number of days per month were adopted from the Julian calendar.

The Julian calendar was regulated by Julius Caesar, Emperor of Rome, in 45 B.C., but it was supposedly created by Romulus, the founder of Rome in about 753 B.C. The Roman calendar started the year with the vernal equinox and consisted of 10 months (Martius, Aprilis, Maius, Junius, Quntilis, Sextilis, September, October, November, and December) for a total of 304 days. The 304 calendar days were followed by an unnamed, unnumbered period in winter. The second king of Rome, Numa Pompilius (715–672 B.C.), introduced January and February between December and March, increasing the length of the year to 354 or 355 days. January has 31 days and is named for Janus, two-headed god of doorways and gates; February has 28 days (or 29 in leap year) and comes from the word *Februarius,* the month of expiation. March has 31 days and is named for Mars, the Roman god of war. April has 30 days and is derived from the Latin verb meaning "to open." May has 31 days and is named for Maia, the goddess of spring and growth. June, with 30 days, is named for Juno, the goddess of wisdom and marriage. July with 31 days is named for Julius

Caesar. August has 31 days and is named for Augustus Caesar. September (originally the seventh month of the calendar) means seven in Latin, and has 30 days. October, with 31 days, means eight in Latin; November is the Latin word for nine and has 30 days; and, December, Latin for ten, has 31 days. Eventually, the Julian calendar became so messy and inaccurate that a change had to be made.

A new calendar was introduced by Pope Gregory XIII in 1582 and was named for him. It consisted of an ordinary year of 365 days and a leap year of 366 days every fourth year. It set the vernal equinox at 21 March. While most of the world changed to the Gregorian calendar in the 1500s, Russia and Greece continued to use the Julian calendar until the 1900s; the Greek Orthodox Church in Russia still uses the Julian calendar. The Gregorian calendar is so accurate that the difference between the calendar and a solar year is now only about 26.3 seconds. This difference will increase 0.52 seconds every hundred years because our solar system is gradually shrinking.

The Hebrew Calendar

The Hebrew calendar is the official calendar of Israel and the liturgical calendar of the Jewish faith. Jews all over the world use the Hebrew calendar for religious purposes. The calendar is a solar/lunar calendar; years are linked to the motion of the earth around the sun, and months are linked to the motions of the moon. The Hebrew calendar is calculated mathematically rather than based on scientific observation.

An ordinary year has 12 months; a leap year has 13 months. The extra month is added every 3rd, 6th, 8th, 11th, 14th, 17th, and 19th year. Every month starts on the day of the new moon. The months and their lengths are: Tishri (30), Heshvan (29), Kislev (29), Tevet (29), Shevat (30), Adar I (30), Adar II (29), Nisan (30), Iyar (29), Sivan (30), Tammuz (29), Av (30), and Elul (29). The month Adar I is only used in leap years; in non-leap years, Adar II is simply called "Adar."

A Hebrew day beings at sunset, and days go from sunset to sunset. An ordinary year has 353, 354, or 355 days. The Jewish New Year begins on 1 Tishri, usually around the autumnal equinox (September 23). Rosh Hashanah, the New Year, celebrates the creation of the world. Jews believe the world was created in 3761 B.C. The Hebrew calendar does not use B.C. and A.D.; instead they use A.M. (amno mundi), which is Latin for "year of the world." They began their calendar with the creation of the world in A.M. 5759.

The Hebrew calendar is the oldest calendar still in use today.

The Islamic Calendar

The Islamic calendar was laid down by Mohammad in the Koran and is used for religious purposes by Muslims in most countries around the Persian Gulf. The Islamic calendar is a lunar calendar with 12 months, each month beginning with the appearance of the crescent moon. Because observation by the naked eye can vary due to weather, location, and other factors, this makes the Islamic calendar difficult to calculate and print in advance. Saudi Arabia doesn't depend on human observation for their calendar, however; they calculate the months mathematically. Religious leaders and scientists disagree whether to rely on observations

Reading Engagement: Grade 8

Name: _____ Date: _____

Level One, Lesson 2: Time After Time (cont.)

(which are subject to error) or to use calculations (which may be based on poor models). The Gregorian calendar is usually used for business and civil matters in Islamic nations.

Months on the Islamic calendar are made up of seven-day weeks. Each day begins at sunset and is specified by a number, with day 1 beginning at sunset on Saturday and ending at sunset on Sunday. Day 5 is called Jum'a and is the day for group prayers. Jum'a begins at sunset on Thursday and ends at sunset on Friday. The months and number of days in the month are: Muharran (30), Safar (29), Rabi' al-awwal (30), Rabi' al-thani (29), Jumada al-awwal (30), Jumada al-thani (29), Rajab (30), Sha'ban (29), Ramadan (30), Shawwal (29), Dhu al-Qi'dah (30), and Dhu al-Hijah (29).

The Islamic year is about 11 days shorter than in the Christian calendar and begins on the vernal equinox (about March 21). Years are counted since the Hijra (Mohammad's emigration to Medina in A.D. 622). In the year A.D. 2003, the Islamic year was 1424. 1,381 years on the Christian calendar have passed since the Hijra (2003 – 622 = 1381), while 1,424 years have passed on the Islamic calendar.

Summary

A calendar is a system for organizing time, and every civilization has, in some way, measured and recorded time. The Islamic calendar is based on the motion of the moon, but the year has no connection to the motion of the earth around the sun. The new year begins on the vernal equinox (around March 21). In the Hebrew calendar, years are linked to the motion of earth around the sun, and months are linked to the motions of the moon. The first day of the new year on the Hebrew calendar is 1 Tishri, the autumnal equinox, (around September 23). The Christian calendar, used by most countries around the world for business and civic purposes and by Christians for liturgical purposes, is based on the motion of the earth around the sun; the months, however, have no connection with the motion of the moon. The new year on the Christian calendar begins 1 January.

© Mark Twain Media, Inc., Publishers

Reading Engagement: Grade 8   Level One, Lesson 2: Time After Time

Name: _____ Date: _____

Level One, Lesson 2: Time After Time (cont.)

Reading Guide for "Time After Time"

BEFORE READING

Before reading "Time After Time," complete the **Before Reading** section of the Reading Guide.

A. Prereading Activity: Connecting Background Knowledge

World Calendar

There are over 40 calendars in current use around the world. Would you be in favor of adopting a world calendar? What would be the advantages and disadvantages of having a world calendar? Discuss in small groups and come to a consensus on the questions.

B. Vocabulary: Meaning

Time Vocabulary

Directions: Arrange the words in the Word Bank in alphabetical order, and then use each word in a sentence that indicates that you know what it means. Use a dictionary, if necessary.

WORD BANK

expiation	millennia	civic	astronomical
vernal equinox	emigration	liturgical	autumnal equinox

1. _____
   _____
   _____

2. _____
   _____
   _____

Reading Engagement: Grade 8 Level One, Lesson 2: Time After Time

Name: _____ Date: _____

Level One, Lesson 2: Time After Time (cont.)

3. _____
   _____
   _____

4. _____
   _____
   _____

5. _____
   _____
   _____

6. _____
   _____
   _____

7. _____
   _____
   _____

8. _____
   _____
   _____

© Mark Twain Media, Inc., Publishers

Reading Engagement: Grade 8   Level One, Lesson 2: Time After Time

Name: _____ Date: _____

Level One, Lesson 2: Time After Time (cont.)

C. Prereading Questions

1. What do you think this reading is going to be about?

   _____

   _____

2. Read the questions in the **After Reading** section of this Reading Guide.

   a. Which question do you find the most interesting?

   _____

   _____

   b. Which answer do you think will be hardest to find?

   _____

   _____

3. What is your purpose for reading this story? Finish this sentence: I am reading to find out ...

   _____

   _____

DURING READING

1. Put a check mark in the margin next to the information that answers the questions in the **After Reading** section.

2. Circle any words you don't know when you come to them in the passage.

3. Put a question mark in the margin for anything you don't understand.

© Mark Twain Media, Inc., Publishers   19

Reading Engagement: Grade 8

Level One, Lesson 2: Time After Time

Name: _____ Date: _____

Level One, Lesson 2: Time After Time (cont.)

AFTER READING

1. **READING THE LINES:** Answer these questions by using information in the selection.

    a. Where did the Islamic calendar originate?

    _____
    _____

    b. When is the New Year on the Islamic calendar?

    _____

    c. On what day do the months begin on the Hebrew calendar?

    _____
    _____

    d. Why did the Christian calendar change from the Julian calendar to the Gregorian calendar?

    _____
    _____
    _____

    e. About how many calendars are in use in the world today?

    _____

2. **READING BETWEEN THE LINES:** Answer these questions by inferring ideas in the selection.

    a. How reliable is the Islamic calendar?

    _____
    _____
    _____

© Mark Twain Media, Inc., Publishers

Level One, Lesson 2: Time After Time (cont.)

    b.   What was the original purpose of the Christian calendar?

    c.   How is the Hebrew calendar based on astronomical events?

    d.   When was the last time the Hebrew calendar had Adar I?

3.   READING BEYOND THE LINES: Answer these questions with your own opinions.

    a.   In what month on the Islamic calendar is your birthday?

    b.   Why was the first month of the year, January, named for Janus, the two-headed god of doorways and gates? What is the connection between the two?

    c.   On the Christian calendar, from where do the names of the months come?

Level One, Lesson 2: Time After Time (cont.)

ASSESSMENT/REINFORCEMENT

There are many other calendars in use today. The Chinese calendar might be the most well-known. Research the history of the Chinese calendar. Use the Chinese Zodiac calendar below to answer these questions:

- In what year were you born? In what years were your parents, brothers, and sisters born?
- Determine what animals are assigned to your family members' birth years. Do any of the animals (and their descriptions) seem relevant to your family members?

	Born in 1924, 1936, 1948, 1960, 1972, 1984, 1996, 2008, …	**RAT:** You are imaginative, charming, and truly generous to the person you love. However, you have a tendency to be quick-tempered and overly critical. You are also inclined to be somewhat of an opportunist. Born under this sign, you should be happy in sales or as a writer, critic, or publicist.
	Born in 1925, 1937, 1949, 1961, 1973, 1985, 1997, 2009, …	**BUFFALO:** A born leader, you inspire confidence from all around you. You are conservative, methodical, and good with your hands. Guard against being chauvinistic and always demanding your own way. The Buffalo would be successful as a skilled surgeon, general, or hairdresser.
	Born in 1926, 1938, 1950, 1962, 1974, 1986, 1998, 2010, …	**TIGER:** You are sensitive, emotional, and capable of great love. However, you have a tendency to get carried away and be stubborn about what you think is right, often seen as a "hothead" or rebel. Your sign shows that you would be excellent as a boss, explorer, race-car driver, or matador.
	Born in 1927, 1939, 1951, 1963, 1975, 1987, 1999, 2011, …	**RABBIT:** You are the kind of person that people like to be around: affectionate, obliging, and always pleasant. However, you have a tendency to get too sentimental and seem superficial. Being cautious and conservative, you are successful in business but would also make a good lawyer, diplomat, or politician.
	Born in 1916, 1928, 1940, 1952, 1964, 1976, 1988, 2000, 2012, …	**DRAGON:** Full of vitality and enthusiasm, the Dragon is a popular individual, even with the reputation of being foolhardy and a bit outspoken at times. You are intelligent, gifted, and a perfectionist, but these qualities make you unduly demanding on others. You would be well-suited to be an artist, priest, or politician.

Level One, Lesson 2: Time After Time (cont.)

	Born in 1917, 1929, 1941, 1953, 1965, 1977, 1989, 2001, 2013, …	**SNAKE:** Rich in wisdom and charm, you are romantic and deep thinking, and your intuition guides you strongly. Avoid procrastination and your stingy attitude towards money. Keep your sense of humor about life. The Snake would be most content as a teacher, philosopher, writer, psychiatrist, or fortuneteller.
	Born in 1918, 1930, 1942, 1954, 1966, 1978, 1990, 2002, 2014, …	**HORSE:** Your capacity for hard work is amazing. You are your own person—very independent. While intelligent and friendly, you have a strong streak of selfishness and sharp cunning and should guard against being egotistical. Your sign suggests success as an adventurer, scientist, poet, or politician.
	Born in 1919, 1931, 1943, 1955, 1967, 1979, 1991, 2003, 2015, …	**GOAT:** Except for the knack of always getting off on the wrong foot with people, the Goat can be charming company. You are elegant and artistic but the first to complain about things. Put aside your pessimism and worry and try to be less dependent on material comforts. You would be best as an actor, gardener, or beachcomber.
	Born in 1920, 1932, 1944, 1956, 1968, 1980, 1992, 2004, 2016, …	**MONKEY:** You are very intelligent and have a clever wit. Because of your extraordinary nature and magnetic personality, you are always well-liked. The Monkey, however, must guard against being an opportunist and distrustful of other people. Your sign promises success in any field you try.
	Born in 1921, 1933, 1945, 1957, 1969, 1981, 1993, 2005, 2017, …	**ROOSTER:** The Rooster is a hard worker, shrewd and definite in decision making, often speaking his mind. Because of this, you tend to seem boastful to others. You are a dreamer, flashy dresser, and extravagant to the extreme. Born under this sign, you should be happy as a restaurant owner, publicist, soldier, or world traveler.
	Born in 1922, 1934, 1946, 1958, 1970, 1982, 1994, 2006, 2018, …	**DOG:** The Dog will never let you down. Born under this sign, you are honest and faithful to those you love. You are plagued by constant worry and a sharp tongue; however, you have a tendency to be a fault finder. You would make an excellent businessperson.
	Born in 1923, 1935, 1947, 1959, 1971, 1983, 1995, 2007, 2019, …	**PIG:** You are a splendid companion, an intellectual with a very strong need to set difficult goals and carry them out. You are sincere, tolerant, and honest, but by expecting the same from others, you are incredibly naive. Your quest for material goods could be your downfall. The Pig would be best in the arts as an entertainer, or possibly a lawyer.

Level One, Lesson 3: Did You Know …?

Did You Know …?

- Scientists can now grow human brain cells in a laboratory dish.
- One out of every four Americans has been on television.
- An albatross seabird can fly as fast as 25 mph while sleeping.
- An average one-dollar bill wears out after 18 months, but it takes a coin, on average, 25 years to wear out.
- White and blue are the most common school colors in the United States.
- Sharks are capable of surviving, on average, six weeks without eating. The record is fifteen months by a "swell shark."
- Millions of nerve signals enter your brain every single second of your life.
- Kobe Bryant, the basketball star, was named after the Kobe Japanese Steakhouse in Pennsylvania.
- Americans eat 18 acres of pizza every day.
- In New Mexico, over eleven thousand people have visited a tortilla chip that appears to have the face of Jesus burned into it.
- In 1998, 8.2 million teenagers ages 16–19 worked. A total of 2.5 million worked full-time, and 5.7 million worked part-time.
- There are 18 different animal shapes in a box of Animal Crackers.
- The King of Hearts is the only king in a deck of playing cards without a mustache.
- There are about 10,000 banks in the U.S., and every day about 20 of them are robbed. The average take is $2,500.
- Americans of all ages list walking as their #1 sports activity. Swimming is #2, and bike riding is #3.
- The sun is 330,330 times the size of the earth.
- The Mall of America in Bloomington, Minnesota, is the nation's largest mall, with over 500 stores.

Level One, Lesson 3: Did You Know ...? (cont.)

- A cockroach can live several weeks with its head cut off before finally dying of starvation.
- In Natoma, Kansas, it is illegal to throw knives at men wearing striped suits.
- 600,000 children eat lunch at school, and 140,000 eat breakfast there.
- Most lipstick contains fish scales.
- Before he became a famous singer, Elvis Presley worked as a truck driver.
- Elvis Presley's records have sold more than 1 billion copies, making him the most successful solo recording artist ever.
- During his lifetime, Walt Disney was nominated for 64 Academy Awards.
- Of the 33 largest cities in the United States, New Orleans has the highest percentage of obese people. More than 37% of its residents are considered obese.
- Beethoven published his first composition when he was only 12 years old.
- The ten most common last names in the United States are: Smith, Johnson, Williams, Brown, Jones, Miller, Davis, Wilson, Anderson, and Taylor.
- The largest organ in your body is your skin. An adult has about 20 square feet of skin.
- Crazy, but true, are these real names of real people: Mac Aroni, Doctor Doctor, Memory Lane, A. Moron, Frank N. Stein, and Cigar Stubbs.

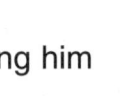

Level One, Lesson 3: Did You Know …? (cont.)

Reading Guide for "Did You Know …?"

BEFORE READING

Before reading "Did You Know …?," complete the **Before Reading** section of the Reading Guide.

A. Prereading Activity: Activating Background Knowledge

Amazing Facts

Directions: Did you know that the singer Tina Turner's real name is Annie Mae Bullock? Did you know that the top-selling video of all time is *The Lion King*? Did you know that in Japan it's considered impolite to show your teeth when laughing? There are so many amazing facts; what facts do you know? Write a few of them here and share them with others.

1. _____
   _____
   _____

2. _____
   _____
   _____

3. _____
   _____
   _____

4. _____
   _____
   _____

Reading Engagement: Grade 8 Level One, Lesson 3: Did You Know ...?

Name: _____ Date: _____

Level One, Lesson 3: Did You Know ...? (cont.)

B. Vocabulary: Multiple Syllables

Syllables

Directions: Here are some multisyllabic vocabulary words from this reading. First tell how many syllables you hear in each word, and then divide the word into syllables. If you get stuck, use a dictionary.

	Word	No. of Syllables	Division of Syllables
1.	Pennsylvania		
2.	laboratory		
3.	television		
4.	albatross		
5.	tortilla		
6.	mustache		
7.	cockroach		
8.	starvation		
9.	Beethoven		
10.	obese		

C. Prereading Questions

1. What do you think this reading is going to be about?

   _____

   _____

2. Read the questions in the **After Reading** section of this Reading Guide.

   a. Which question do you find the most interesting?

   _____

   _____

Reading Engagement: Grade 8   Level One, Lesson 3: Did You Know ...?

Name: _____   Date: _____

Level One, Lesson 3: Did You Know ...? (cont.)

b. Which answer do you think will be hardest to find?

_____

_____

3. What is your purpose for reading this story? Finish this sentence: I am reading to find out ...

_____

_____

DURING READING

1. Put a check mark in the margin next to the information that answers the questions in the **After Reading** section.

2. Circle any words you don't know when you come to them in the passage.

3. Put a question mark in the margin for anything you don't understand.

AFTER READING

1. READING THE LINES: Answer these questions by using information in the selection.

   a. What is so unusual about sharks?

   _____

   _____

   _____

   b. Why are people in New Mexico flocking to see a tortilla chip?

   _____

   _____

   _____

© Mark Twain Media, Inc., Publishers

Level One, Lesson 3: Did You Know ...? (cont.)

c. Which major U.S. city has the highest percentage of obese people?

d. Where is the largest mall in the United States?

2. READING BETWEEN THE LINES: Answer these questions by inferring ideas in the selection.

   a. In your opinion, which is the most fascinating fact in the reading selection?

   b. Why do you think walking is listed as the #1 fitness activity in the United States?

   c. What percentage of U.S. banks are robbed on any given day?

   d. What are your school colors?

Reading Engagement: Grade 8　　　　　　　　　　　Level One, Lesson 3: Did You Know …?

Name: _____ Date: _____

Level One, Lesson 3: Did You Know …? (cont.)

3. READING BEYOND THE LINES: Answer these questions with your own opinions.

   a. Do you know anyone with a real but "crazy" name? Who?

   _____

   _____

   _____

   b. What are some of the common last names of people you know?

   _____

   _____

   _____

ASSESSMENT/REINFORCEMENT

A. Check out these websites to find new fantastic facts. Make a bulletin board out of the facts you find.

   www.factmonster.com

   www.timeforkids.com

   www.goofball.com

Reading Engagement: Grade 8   Level One, Lesson 3: Did You Know ...?

Name: _____ Date: _____

Level One, Lesson 3: Did You Know ...? (cont.)

B.   Did You Know ...? Crossword Puzzle: Complete the crossword puzzle using the clues below and information from the reading.

ACROSS
1. One out of every four Americans has been on _____.
5. The largest organ in the human body is its _____.
7. An _____ can fly as fast as 25 mph while sleeping.
11. Scientists can now grow _____ _____ _____ in a laboratory dish.
12. The _____ is 330,330 times the size of the earth.
13. Elvis Presley is the most successful _____ recording artist ever.
15. Most _____ contains fish scales.
16. During his lifetime, _____ _____ was nominated for 64 Academy Awards.

DOWN
1. In New Mexico, over eleven thousand people have visited a _____ _____ that appears to have the face of Jesus burned into it.
2. In Natoma, Kansas, it is illegal to throw knives at men wearing _____ _____.
3. _____ _____ has the highest percentage of obese people of the 33 largest cities in the U.S.
4. Americans eat 18 acres of _____ every day.
6. _____ are capable of surviving, on average, six weeks without eating.
8. White and blue are the most common _____ _____ in the United States.
9. There are 18 different _____ shapes in a box of Animal Crackers.
10. Millions of _____ signals enter your brain every single second of your life.
11. The King of _____ is the only king in a deck of playing cards without a mustache.
13. A cockroach can live several weeks with its head cut off before finally dying of _____.
14. Americans of all ages list _____ as their #1 sports activity.

© Mark Twain Media, Inc., Publishers   31

Level Two, Lesson 1: NASCAR

NASCAR

One of the most popular sports today is automobile racing, especially NASCAR racing. Thousands of fans flock to racing venues, coolers and picnic lunches in hand, to watch million-dollar stock cars race around a track. To learn more about NASCAR, read the Q & A below.

Q: What does NASCAR stand for?
A: Stock car racing was organized and systematized by Bill France, Sr., who founded the National Association of Stock Car Auto Racing (NASCAR) in 1947. Prior to this time, stock car racing was disorganized and full of uncertainty. Drivers and their teams never knew from day to day whether track owners could pay the winning drivers or whether there would even be enough drivers to hold a race. France changed all that by setting parameters and instituting a list of rules that ensured that cars would be virtually the same.

Q: What are those stickers all over the cars?
A: The stickers advertise the car's sponsors. NASCAR racing is very expensive. Experts estimate that it takes more than $15 million per year to run a top 10 team on the NASCAR circuit. The average race mechanic makes $50,000 per year in salary, plus benefits, and most teams employ about 40 people. It costs between $80,000 and $150,000 to prepare for, enter, and travel to each race. Each car costs more than $100,000, and many teams keep at least ten cars on hand at any given time. Tires can cost more than half a million dollars per year. Top sponsors pay between $3 and $6 million per year to display their names prominently on a car; additional sponsors pay to have a sticker (much smaller than the sponsor's name) slapped on the car and a patch sewn on the driver's coveralls.

Q: What is a pit stop, and what happens there?
A: A good pit stop is completed in less than 20 seconds and includes a full tank of gas and four fresh tires. When the driver pulls into the pit, three men sprint around to the passenger side of the car. One man lifts the car with a pneumatic jack while the other two loosen the lug nuts on the tire. They then get fresh tires from the tire carriers and put them into place. Sprinting, the three men shift around the back of the car and repeat the procedure on the other side. While that is happening, the gas man fills the tank, another cleans the windshield and grill, and another makes sure the driver gets a drink of water. A good pit stop crew can make the difference between first and second place.

Level Two, Lesson 1: NASCAR (cont.)

Q: How are points awarded for each race?

A: In NASCAR the teams race every week toward the end-of-the-year championship—the NASCAR NEXTEL Cup. Every race is worth the same number of points; there are no "unimportant" races. The winner of each NASCAR race receives 180 points. The runner-up in each event scores 170. From there the point total decreases by five points, then four points, then three points, down to the last-place driver who gets 34 points. Five bonus points are given to any drivers who lead a lap, and an additional bonus of five points is given to the driver who leads the most laps. Following the twenty-sixth race of the season, all drivers in NASCAR's Top 10 and any others within 400 points of the leader qualify to race in the "Chase for the Championship." All drivers in the "Chase" will have their point totals adjusted, with the season's first-place driver receiving 5,050 points; the second-place driver will start with 5,045 points and so on, with five-point incremental drops continuing down the list of contenders.

Q: What do the colored flags during the race mean?

A: There are eight different flags that the NASCAR officials use to control the race. The green flag signals the beginning of the race and is used after a caution period to tell drivers that the track is clear, and the race can continue. The yellow flag is the caution signal that there is a hazard on the track. It signals the drivers to slow down and stay behind the pace car. The yellow flag is signaled when there has been an accident or when there is light rain or debris on the track. It is also used when an emergency vehicle needs to cross the track or when a person or animal is on the track. The white flag means there is just one more lap to go in the race; the white flag is used only once in a race. The checkered flag signals that the race is over. The driver who is the first one to receive the checkered flag is the winner. The red flag means that all cars must come to a stop and includes both the drivers and the pit crews. The red flag is used for a rain delay, when the track is blocked because of emergency vehicles, or a particularly bad accident has occurred. The red flag is always followed by a few yellow laps so the drivers have a chance to warm up their engines and pit if they need to. The black flag is the "consultation" flag. The driver who receives the black flag must pit to respond to a NASCAR concern. The black flag is given to a driver who breaks a rule, such as breaking the speed limit on pit road, or to a driver whose car is smoking or dropping pieces on the racetrack, or to a driver who is not going fast enough for the race. A driver who receives a black flag must pit within five laps. A black flag with a white X is given to a driver who receives a black flag and does NOT pit within five laps. This

Level Two, Lesson 1: NASCAR (cont.)

flag tells the driver he is no longer being scored by NASCAR and has been disqualified from the race. The blue flag with diagonal orange stripe is a "courtesy" flag that means "move over." It is the only flag that a driver can ignore if he chooses. The blue flag is used to let the drivers know that the leaders are coming up behind them and that they should be courteous and move over to let the leaders race. While it is optional, NASCAR frowns on anyone who repeatedly ignores this request.

Q: Who are some of the best drivers in NASCAR today?
A: Dale Earnhardt was probably the most talented driver in the history of NASCAR racing. He won Rookie of the Year in 1979 and followed it by winning the series championship in 1980. He earned 76 series wins, ranking him sixth on NASCAR's all-time wins list. He won $41,538,362 racing and is the all-time race winner at Daytona. Earnhardt was a five-time winner of the National Motorsports Press Association's Driver of the Year award and two-time winner of the American Driver of the Year award. Dale Earnhardt died in 2001 in Daytona doing what he loved, racing. Dale Earnhardt, Junior, seems to be following in his father's big footsteps. Voted the most popular driver in 2003, Junior has nine career victories. He is a third-generation NASCAR champion following his father, Dale, Sr., and his grandfather, Ralph. Jeff Gordon is another talented driver; he has won four NASCAR Winston Cup Series championships, 52 NASCAR Winston/NEXTEL Cup Series victories, 34 NASCAR Winston/NEXTEL Cup Series pole positions, and the 1993 NASCAR Winston Cup Rookie of the Year Award. Tony Stewart and Jimmy Johnson are also gifted drivers on the NEXTEL circuit.

Q: Have there ever been any woman drivers?
A: Yes, Janet Guthrie gained fame by competing on the Winston Cup circuit in the late 1970s and early 1980s, and Shawna Robinson won the AC Delco 100 in Asheville, North Carolina, in 1988. They were not the first women behind the wheel of a stock car. A woman started thirteenth and finished fourteenth in the very first NASCAR race ever run. Sarah Christian, Louise Smith, and Ethel Mobley have driven the 166-mile race at Daytona Beach. Christian finished sixth and Mobley eleventh, and Smith twentieth after suffering an early roll-over in the race.

Level Two, Lesson 1: NASCAR (cont.)

Reading Guide for "NASCAR"

BEFORE READING

Before reading "NASCAR," complete the **Before Reading** section of the Reading Guide.

A. Prereading Activity: Assessing Background Knowledge

NASCAR Clues

1. What do these have in common?
    Daytona 500
    Coca-Cola 600
    Winston Select 500
    Mountain Dew Southern 500

_____

2. What do these have in common?
    M & M's
    U.S. Army
    Budweiser
    Home Depot

_____

3. What do these have in common?
    #38
    #8
    #20
    #24

_____

4. What do these have in common?
    Kurt Busch
    Jimmy Johnson
    Tony Stewart
    Bobby Labonte

_____

Reading Engagement: Grade 8   Level Two, Lesson 1: NASCAR

Name: _____   Date: _____

Level Two, Lesson 1: NASCAR (cont.)

B. Vocabulary: Definitions

Directions: Answer the following questions about these vocabulary words.

Vocabulary

1. What does *parameter* mean?

   _____

   _____

2. What does *ensured* mean?

   _____

   _____

3. What does *incremental* mean?

   _____

   _____

4. What does *debris* mean?

   _____

   _____

5. What does *coveralls* mean?

   _____

   _____

C. Prereading Questions

1. What do you think this reading is going to be about?

   _____

   _____

© Mark Twain Media, Inc., Publishers   36

Level Two, Lesson 1: NASCAR (cont.)

2. Read the questions in the **After Reading** section of this Reading Guide.

   a. Which question do you find the most interesting?

   _____
   _____

   b. Which answer do you think will be hardest to find?

   _____
   _____

3. What is your purpose for reading this story? Finish this sentence: I am reading to find out ...

   _____
   _____

DURING READING

1. Put a check mark in the margin next to the information that answers the questions in the **After Reading** section.

2. Circle any words you don't know when you come to them in the passage.

3. Put a question mark in the margin for anything you don't understand.

AFTER READING

1. READING THE LINES: Answer these questions by using information in the selection.

   a. What does NASCAR stand for?

   _____
   _____

Level Two, Lesson 1: NASCAR (cont.)

b. About how much does it cost to race on the NASCAR circuit?

_____

_____

c. What does it mean if a driver receives the black flag with a white X?

_____

_____

_____

d. Name two people currently racing on the NASCAR circuit.

_____

2. READING BETWEEN THE LINES: Answer these questions by inferring ideas in the selection.

   a. If there were six races a year, about how much would it cost to prepare for, enter, and travel to the six races?

   _____

   _____

   b. Could a driver who *does not* win the final race be declared the champion? How?

   _____

   _____

   _____

   c. Could a woman be a NASCAR driver? Why or why not?

   _____

   _____

   _____

Reading Engagement: Grade 8   Level Two, Lesson 1: NASCAR

Name: _____ Date: _____

Level Two, Lesson 1: NASCAR (cont.)

   d.   What is a good pit stop, and what happens during one?

   _____

   _____

   _____

3. READING BEYOND THE LINES: Answer these questions with your own opinions.

   a.   Do you know the sponsors of these popular cars?

        #48   _____

        #24   _____

        #8   _____

   b.   Have you ever watched a NASCAR race? Did you enjoy it? Why or why not?

   _____

   _____

   _____

   c.   Why do you think NASCAR is so popular?

   _____

   _____

   _____

ASSESSMENT/REINFORCEMENT

A.   Watch a NASCAR race and keep track of the number and color of the flags used in the race. Note the cars and drivers in the race, especially those who come in first through fifth. Give an oral report to your classmates. Check out NASCAR at www. nascar.com.

© Mark Twain Media, Inc., Publishers

Reading Engagement: Grade 8   Level Two, Lesson 1: NASCAR

Name: _____ Date: _____

Level Two, Lesson 1: NASCAR (cont.)

B. Stock Car Words and Terms: Place the letter of the definition in the second column on the blank next to the corresponding term in the first column. Use the reading selection, the Internet, or other reference sources if you need help.

_____ 1. hauler
_____ 2. drag
_____ 3. broadsided
_____ 4. lap
_____ 5. tachometer
_____ 6. spoiler
_____ 7. drafting
_____ 8. pace car
_____ 9. pole position
_____ 10. groove
_____ 11. checkered flag
_____ 12. caution flag
_____ 13. green flag
_____ 14. set up
_____ 15. pit

A. The yellow flag used to warn drivers of danger on the course
B. The shortest, fastest, and safest route around a track
C. During a race, a disabled car gets hit on the driver's side by another car; also called getting "T-boned"
D. The huge tractor-trailer that transports race cars, along with spare parts, equipment, and supplies; also called a transporter
E. The flag that signals the start of a race and that the course is clear
F. The car that leads the field of competitors through the pace lap and parade lap
G. One complete circuit of the racetrack
H. The area just off the track where cars are refueled, repaired, and tires are changed during a race
I. A flag that signals a driver that he is the winner of the race
J. In a race, the starting position in the front row closest to the infield
K. To follow close behind another car at high speed to take advantage of the reduced air resistance
L. The long, narrow, metal plate mounted on the car's rear deck that breaks up the flow of air and creates traction
M. To prepare a car for a race through the adjustment of various components, such as shock absorbers, springs, etc.
N. Anything that works to retard the car's forward motion
O. A dashboard instrument that reports the revolutions per minute (rpm) of the car's engine

Level Two, Lesson 2: Titanic of the Sky

Titanic of the Sky: The *Hindenburg* Disaster

At 7:25 P.M. on May 6, 1937, the pride of the German Third Reich, the *Hindenburg,* while attempting to land at Lakehurst Naval Air Station in New Jersey, suddenly burst into flames and crashed to the ground. Out of 97 people aboard, 13 passengers and 22 crew members were killed in the crash. One man on the ground was killed as well. The cause of the fiery crash was not immediately known.

The *Hindenburg* was a marvel of zeppelin design; her sheer size was truly an engineering masterpiece. The colossal airship was 882 feet long and 135.1 feet in diameter (only 78 feet shorter than the *Titanic*)—the largest aircraft to <u>ever</u> fly! It was filled with 7,062,100 cubic feet of hydrogen. The frame was made of an alloy of aluminum and copper with traces of magnesium, manganese, iron, and silicon. Today this alloy is commonly known as duralumin. The *Hindenburg* was powered by four 16-cylinder diesel engines, two per side.

German engineers designed a dirigible that could travel faster than any ship of its day. They pioneered the first transatlantic air service as a "flying hotel." The zeppelin carried passengers inside her huge hull instead of from a protruding gondola section. The Control Car was divided into three areas: the Control Room and Bridge, the Navigation Room, and the cramped Crew Quarters, which were located toward the rear of the airship. The Officers' Mess was a comfortable place for officers to relax while not on duty, and it contained a large bank of windows to allow a view of the earth passing below. Passenger cabins were about 78 x 66 inches and were equipped with an upper and lower bunk, folding wash basin, collapsible writing table, and a device to signal the steward when needed. Compared to the luxurious accommodations on steamships, the accommodations on the *Hindenburg* were quite plain.

The passenger section of the airship had a lounge decorated with a large wall mural that traced the path of great explorations, and it contained a baby grand piano. The Reading and Writing Room was a quiet place where passengers could read or write letters or postcards on special *Hindenburg* stationery. Oddly enough, a passenger ship loaded with an incredibly flammable gas also had a smoking room. The room was built with an anti-chamber airlock that would keep any flames from spreading to the rest of the ship. The room was lined with asbestos, and only one lighter sat at a central table attached with a cord. After all lighters and matches were removed from passengers and locked away, this was the only source of flame available on the whole ship with which to light a cigarette.

The Promenade was the place where passengers spent most of their time. It featured a huge bank of windows and comfortable seating, which allowed passengers a spectacular view of the earth

Level Two, Lesson 2: Titanic of the Sky (cont.)

passing below. Adjacent to the Promenade was the Dining Room, which accommodated 50 passengers in one sitting.

The *Hindenburg* was a thrilling sight. Almost three football fields long, it could fly at 84 miles an hour. Gigantic Nazi swastikas were painted on the tail fins. People everywhere dropped what they were doing to look up at the *Hindenburg* and watch it pass overhead.

On May 6, the *Hindenburg*, having come all the way from Europe, prepared to land at Lakehurst Naval Air Station in New Jersey. Hundreds of family, friends, newspapermen, and onlookers waited at Lakehurst for the *Hindenburg* to land. A radio announcer described how beautiful the ship looked against the night sky, when suddenly a tongue of flame shot out of the stern. The flames spread rapidly, and within just a few seconds, the zeppelin was engulfed in a huge ball of fire. The ship fell tail-first with flames shooting out of it everywhere. It crashed to the ground 32 seconds after the first flame was spotted. The suddenness of the disaster was shocking.

There have been a number of different theories about why the *Hindenburg* exploded. One theory was that the zeppelin was sabotaged—that someone had planted a bomb on board to discredit the Nazi regime. Another was that the ship had been hit by a bolt of lightning; a third theory purported that it was simply an accident. The most credible theory was put forth by Addison Bain, a retired NASA engineer and hydrogen expert. He found proof that neither hydrogen in the hull nor a bomb was to blame. Bain believed the fabric of the *Hindenburg's* outer skin and a new protective coating burned like dry autumn leaves from a single spark of static electricity. In other words, an electrostatic spark caught the extremely flammable skin of the ship on fire, causing the hydrogen to further fuel the flames.

Thirty-six people died as a result of the crash. Hundreds of people on the ground were horrified as they watched the giant airship burn. A radio announcer shouted, "It's burst into flames ... Get out of the way, please, oh my, this is terrible, oh my, get out of the way, please ... Oh, the humanity and all the passengers!" The "infallible" German engineers had designed a flying bomb just waiting to explode. The crash of the *Hindenburg* was truly one of man's worst catastrophic catastrophes.

Level Two, Lesson 2: Titanic of the Sky (cont.)

Reading Guide for "Titanic of the Sky"

BEFORE READING

Before reading "Titanic of the Sky," complete the **Before Reading** section of the Reading Guide.

A. Prereading Activity: Assessing Background Knowledge

Directions: Examine the drawing of a zeppelin below. Write all the things you might know about a zeppelin on and around the drawing. Compare what you've written with that of others and add information, if applicable.

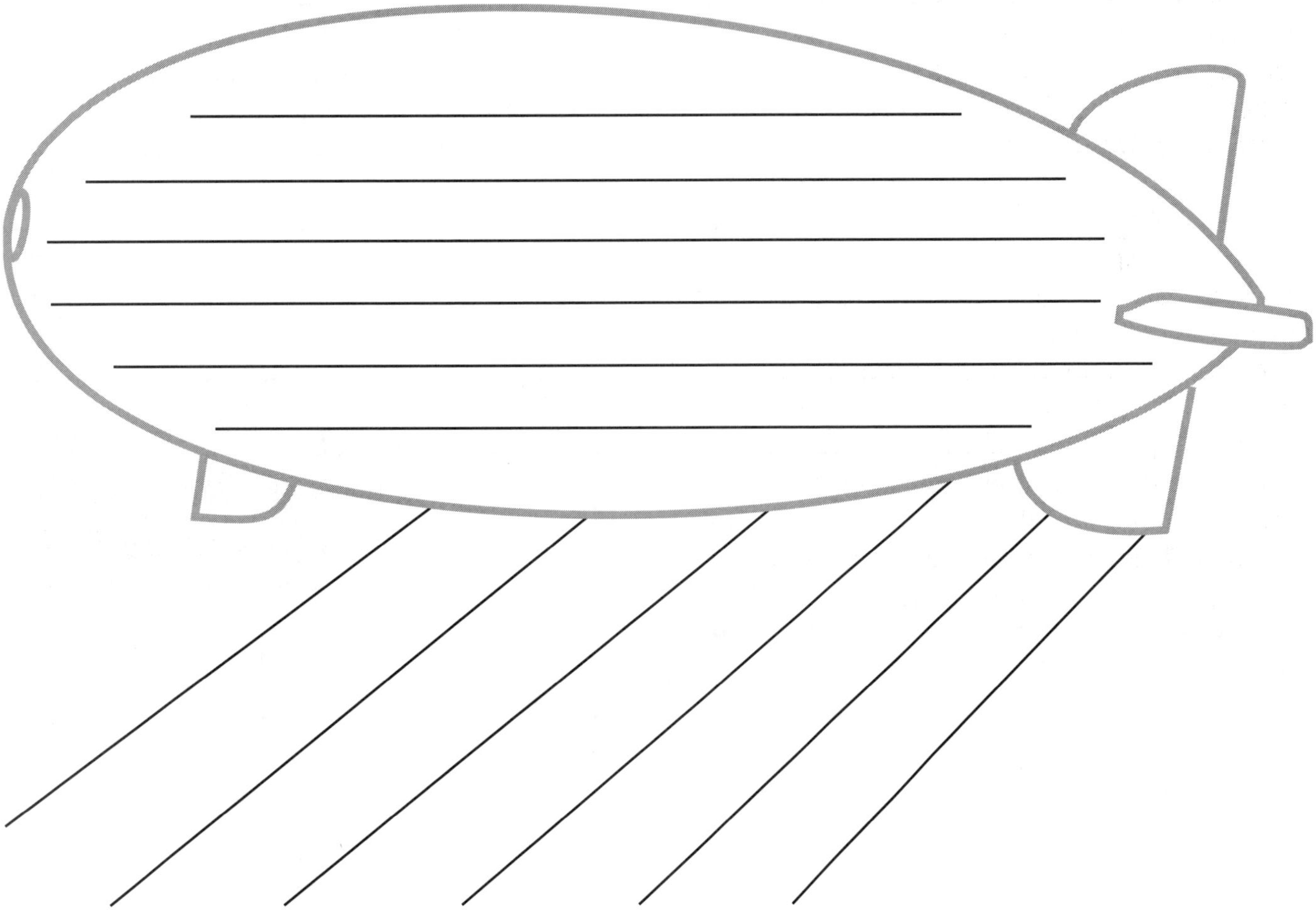

Reading Engagement: Grade 8 | Level Two, Lesson 2: Titanic of the Sky

Name: _____ Date: _____

Level Two, Lesson 2: Titanic of the Sky (cont.)

B. Vocabulary: Word Meanings

Titanic Words

Directions: Define these vocabulary words as they are used in the reading.

1. zeppelin _____
   _____

2. colossal _____
   _____

3. alloy _____
   _____

4. transatlantic _____
   _____

5. dirigible _____
   _____

6. hull _____
   _____

C. Prereading Questions

1. What do you think this reading is going to be about?
   _____
   _____

Level Two, Lesson 2: Titanic of the Sky (cont.)

2. Read the questions in the **After Reading** section of this Reading Guide.

   a. Which question do you find the most interesting?

   _____

   _____

   b. Which answer do you think will be hardest to find?

   _____

   _____

3. What is your purpose for reading this story? Finish this sentence: I am reading to find out ...

   _____

   _____

DURING READING

1. Put a check mark in the margin next to the information that answers the questions in the **After Reading** section.

2. Circle any words you don't know when you come to them in the passage.

3. Put a question mark in the margin for anything you don't understand.

AFTER READING

1. READING THE LINES: Answer these questions by using information in the selection.

   a. What synonyms for the *Hindenburg* does the author use?

   _____

   _____

Level Two, Lesson 2: Titanic of the Sky (cont.)

b. What rooms were included in the passenger section?

_____

_____

_____

c. What was the Promenade?

_____

_____

d. Why was the disastrous crash so shocking?

_____

_____

_____

2. READING BETWEEN THE LINES: Answer these questions by inferring ideas in the selection.

   a. What was the German Third Reich?

   _____

   _____

   _____

   b. What is a steward? What does a steward do?

   _____

   _____

   _____

   _____

Level Two, Lesson 2: Titanic of the Sky (cont.)

    c. Why was it dangerous to smoke on the *Hindenburg*?

    d. What does *catastrophic catastrophe* mean?

3. READING BEYOND THE LINES: Answer these questions with your own opinions.

    a. Besides the cigarettes and lighter, what else was dangerous in the Smoking Room?

    b. Why was the *Hindenburg* such a thrilling sight?

    c. What are some other catastrophic catastrophes?

Reading Engagement: Grade 8

Level Two, Lesson 2: Titanic of the Sky

Name: _____ Date: _____

Level Two, Lesson 2: Titanic of the Sky (cont.)

ASSESSMENT/REINFORCEMENT

A. There are several websites that have pictures and video of the *Hindenburg's* crash. Check them out.

      www.otr.com/hindenburg.html
      www.unmuseum.mus.pa.us/hindenburg.htm
      www.vidicom-tv.com/tohiburg.htm

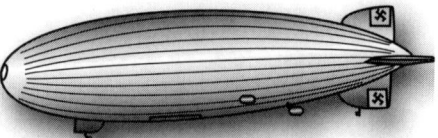

B. Use the clues below to fill in the blanks. Then place the circled letters on the blanks at the bottom of the page to find the hidden word.

1. The ruling party in Germany in the 1930s   ___ ___ Ⓞ ___

2. A huge airship only 78 feet shorter than the *Titanic*
   ___ ___ ___ Ⓞ ___ ___ ___ ___

3. Area with a huge bank of windows and comfortable seating
   Ⓞ ___ ___ ___ ___ ___ ___ ___

4. This may have caught the flammable skin of the ship on fire.   ___ Ⓞ ___ ___ ___

5. Person who takes care of the needs of people onboard the ship
   ___ ___ Ⓞ ___ ___ ___

6. A substance used to prevent the spread of fire that we now know causes lung disease
   ___ ___ ___ ___ ___ ___ ___ ___

7. Incapable of failing   ___ ___ ___ ___ Ⓞ ___ ___ ___ ___

8. Another name for a zeppelin   ___ ___ ___ Ⓞ ___ ___ ___ ___ ___

9. State where the *Hindenburg* crashed   Ⓞ ___ ___ ___ ___ ___ ___ ___

10. Flammable gas inside the *Hindenburg*   ___ ___ ___ ___ ___ ___ ___

Hidden Word: ___ ___ ___ ___ ___ ___ ___

© Mark Twain Media, Inc., Publishers

Level Two, Lesson 3: Lord Stanley's Cup

Lord Stanley's Cup

The Stanley Cup is a trophy given to the best hockey team of the year. It is awarded each year by the National Hockey League (NHL) to the champion of its playoff tournament. More than 100 years old, the Stanley Cup is the oldest trophy that can be won by professional athletes in North America. It is the only professional sports trophy on which the name of every member of the winning team is inscribed and which is passed from player to player before it resides in the NHL Hall of Fame. The Stanley Cup symbolizes professional hockey supremacy.

The Cup isn't really a cup; it is a gold-lined silver bowl measuring $7\frac{1}{2}$ inches high and $11\frac{1}{2}$ inches across. Almost from the beginning, Cup winners began scratching their initials on the cup with nails and knives. From the 1890s to the 1930s, various bands were added to the bottom of the bowl to hold the names (professionally etched) of the winning teams and their players. These bands were later replaced by uneven bands in the 1940s. Today the Cup consists of a bowl, three tiered bands, a collar, and five uniform bands. The trophy stands $35\frac{1}{4}$ inches tall and weighs $34\frac{1}{2}$ pounds.

There are actually two Stanley Cups. The original was retired in 1969 because it became too fragile and damaged easily; it is in the Hockey Hall of Fame in Toronto. The replica is given to the best professional team in the League. The Cup contains not only the names of the winning team and its players but also coaches, management, and club staff. It takes 13 years to fill the ring of the Stanley Cup with names. The bottom ring will be retired after the names of the 2005 champions are inscribed (unless a strike prevents a championship from taking place). One ring has already been retired to the Hall of Fame.

The original Stanley Cup was donated in 1892 by Sir Frederick Arthur, Lord Stanley of Preston and son of the Earl of Derby. Lord Stanley purchased the trophy for 10 guineas ($50 at that time). It was to be presented to the champion hockey club of the Dominion of Canada. Lord Stanley, the Governor General of Canada, became enamored with ice hockey after attending a thrilling exhibition game between the Montreal Victorias and the Montreal Amateur Athletic Association. The whole Stanley family became avid hockey fans; three of his sons played hockey for the Ottawa Rideau Rebels, and two daughters were also involved with the game. One of his daughters, Lady Isabel Stanley, laced up her skates and played for a ladies' hockey team.

Lord Stanley thought hockey needed a trophy for which teams from all over Canada could compete. "I have for some time been thinking that it should be a good thing if there

Level Two, Lesson 3: Lord Stanley's Cup (cont.)

were a challenge cup which should be held from year to year by the champion hockey team in the Dominion of Canada." He purchased the silver "cup" that became known thereafter as the Stanley Cup. Lord Stanley appointed two Ottawa gentlemen to act as the Cup's trustees. Lord Stanley also outlined some rules for the annual competition, the most important of which stipulates that the winners had to return the Cup in good condition. In 1893, the Montreal Amateur Athletic Association hockey club won the first Stanley Cup. Lord Stanley, however, was not present to witness or award the trophy that bears his name. He was called back to England in the middle of the 1893 season.

In 1910, professional teams from the National Hockey Association began to take part in the quest for the trophy. The Portland Rosebuds was the first American team to compete in the Stanley Cup Finals, and the Seattle Metropolitans was the first American team to win the Cup. When the Western Canada Hockey League disbanded in 1926, the Stanley Cup became the championship trophy of the National Hockey League, and Lord Stanley became a charter member of the Hockey Hall of Fame.

The Cup has been awarded every year since 1893 (except for 1919). During the playoffs in 1918–1919 between the Montreal Canadiens and Seattle, a number of players contracted the flu. When five players were hospitalized and one player died, the League cancelled the playoffs after five games. The Montreal Canadiens have won the most Stanley Cups (24); the Toronto Maple Leafs is second with 13. The U.S. team with the most wins is the Detroit Red Wings with 10, and the Red Wings was the first team to win back-to-back titles (in 1936 and 1937).

There are many traditions associated with the Stanley Cup. Perhaps the most cherished dictates that the captain of the winning team receives the Cup first and then hoists it overhead; the cup is then hoisted by each member of the team as they skate around the rink. Another tradition prescribed is that the winning team drinks champagne from the bowl after their victory. Each time the trophy is presented, a summer of celebration begins for the championship team; each player and staff member gets to keep the Cup for 24 hours. The Cup has had a number of misadventures while being passed from player to player. A member of the 1905 Ottawa Silver Seven tried to drop-kick the Cup across the frozen Rideau Canal. Members of the 1924 Canadiens left it by a roadside after repairing a flat tire on their way to celebrate their win at owner Leo Dandurand's home. Sylvain Lefebvre of the 1996 Colorado Avalanche had his daughter baptized in it, and New York Islanders' Brian Trottier used the bowl as a food dish for his dog.

The Stanley Cup travels about 250 days per year and has been to Russia, Japan, Switzerland, the Czech Republic, Sweden, Finland, and the Bahamas. It has appeared on "The Late Show" with David Letterman, "The Tonight Show" with Jay Leno, "Meet the Press" with Tim Russert, "The Late Late Show" with Craig Kilborn, and "Late Night" with Conan O'Brien. The Stanley Cup has been on a roller coaster at Universal Studios theme park, at the "Hollywood" sign in Los Angeles, on the back of a motorcycle, and in an igloo in Rankin Inlet. The Stanley Cup has been a guest at the White House twice, once as the guest of George Herbert Bush and once as the guest of Bill Clinton.

The legend and glory of the Stanley Cup live in the dreams of hockey players and fans alike. The trophy represents the best in hockey and is coveted by each team in the National Hockey League. Though purchased by a lord, the Stanley Cup is a trophy of the people.

Reading Engagement: Grade 8　　　　　　　　　　　　Level Two, Lesson 3: Lord Stanley's Cup

Name: _____　Date: _____

Level Two, Lesson 3: Lord Stanley's Cup (cont.)

Reading Guide for "Lord Stanley's Cup"

BEFORE READING

Before reading "Lord Stanley's Cup," complete the **Before Reading** section of the Reading Guide.

A. Prereading Activity: Activating Background Knowledge

Pretest

Directions: Examine the drawing, and then answer the questions to the best of your ability.

1. What is the object in the drawing?

   _____

   _____

2. What is the name of the object?

   _____

   _____

3. For what is it used?

   _____

   _____

© Mark Twain Media, Inc., Publishers　　　51

Reading Engagement: Grade 8

Level Two, Lesson 3: Lord Stanley's Cup (cont.)

B. Vocabulary: Meaning

Hockey Vocabulary

Directions: Match the word in Column A with the correct definition in Column B.

Column A

_____ 1. inscribe
_____ 2. supremacy
_____ 3. etch
_____ 4. tiered
_____ 5. enamored
_____ 6. trustees
_____ 7. quest
_____ 8. cherish
_____ 9. hoist
_____ 10. champagne

Column B

A. to write with a laser or drill
B. fascinated
C. people trusted with something
D. a search
E. engrave
F. arranged in rows or layers
G. the highest power
H. lift or raise
I. to hold dear
J. a sparkling white wine

C. Prereading Questions

1. What do you think this reading is going to be about?

   _____

   _____

2. Read the questions in the **After Reading** section of this Reading Guide.

   a. Which question do you find the most interesting?

   _____

   _____

Level Two, Lesson 3: Lord Stanley's Cup (cont.)

    b.   Which answer do you think will be hardest to find?

_____

_____

3. What is your purpose for reading this story? Finish this sentence: I am reading to find out ...

_____

_____

DURING READING

1. Put a check mark in the margin next to the information that answers the questions in the **After Reading** section.

2. Circle any words you don't know when you come to them in the passage.

3. Put a question mark in the margin for anything you don't understand.

AFTER READING

1. READING THE LINES: Answer these questions by using information in the selection.

    a.   What is the Stanley Cup?

_____

_____

    b.   To whom is it given?

_____

_____

Level Two, Lesson 3: Lord Stanley's Cup (cont.)

c. When is it given?

2. READING BETWEEN THE LINES: Answer these questions by inferring ideas in the selection.

   a. In what ways is the Stanley Cup not like other trophies?

   b. Besides the Stanley Cup, what are some other things that stand about 35–36 inches tall?

   c. Was the Dominion of Canada an independent country in the 1800s? If not, to what country did it belong?

3. READING BEYOND THE LINES: Answer these questions with your own opinions.

   a. How valuable is the Stanley Cup today?

   b. Name a team that has recently won the Cup.

Level Two, Lesson 3: Lord Stanley's Cup (cont.)

c. Should girls be allowed to play hockey on boys' teams? Why or why not?

_____

_____

_____

d. What is your favorite hockey team?

_____

ASSESSMENT/REINFORCEMENT

A. Watch the Stanley Cup finals of the National Hockey League to see if the traditions are upheld by the winning club.

B. If the statement is true, circle the "T." If the statement is false, circle the "F."

T F 1. Except for a few public appearances, the Stanley Cup is always kept in the Hockey Hall of Fame.

T F 2. It takes 13 years to fill the ring of the Stanley Cup with names.

T F 3. Originally, the Stanley Cup was only awarded to Canadian teams.

T F 4. Lord Stanley first presented the Cup to the Montreal Amateur Athletic Association in 1893.

T F 5. Every member of the winning team has his name engraved on the ring of the Stanley Cup.

T F 6. The original Stanley Cup was lost in the Rideau Canal.

T F 7. Each player and staff member of the winning team gets to keep the Cup for 24 hours.

T F 8. Today, the Stanley Cup is the championship trophy of the National Hockey League.

Reading Engagement: Grade 8   Level Three, Lesson 1: American Royalty, Part I

Name: _____ Date: _____

Level Three, Lesson 1: American Royalty, Part I

American Royalty, Part I

"Aloha, e komo mai."

Which state in the United States once had a royal family living in a royal palace? If you guessed Hawaii, you are correct. Hawaii is the only U.S. state to have had a kingdom with its own monarchy and is the only state with real royal palaces. The Hawaiian monarchy began in 1790 when a local chief, Kamehameha the Great, took power by defeating the numerous chiefs who ruled the different areas across the seven main Hawaiian Islands. Kamehameha was the first royal, and Queen Liliuokalani was the last. For nearly a hundred years in between, the royal families ruled the hearts and minds of the Hawaiian people through a system of Hawaiian temples and chiefs. The Hawaiian monarchy was replaced by an American-style government brought about by a coup of unscrupulous non-Hawaiian businessmen.

King Kamehameha ruled Hawaii from 1790 to 1819. According to legend, a bright star (Halley's Comet?) appeared in the sky when he was born in 1758. Believing that the star portended the birth of a fearsome conqueror, his grandfather, a high chief at the time, ordered all male infants killed in the hope of eliminating any possibility of a so-called "chosen child." Kamehameha was secretly rescued and brought up in isolation; Kamehameha means "the lonely one."

As an adult, Kamehameha became chief of the northern half of the island of Hawaii. He was a bold and brilliant warrior who subsequently conquered and united the rest of the Hawaiian Islands. King Kamehameha had many wives, which was the custom of the royalty at the time. His favorite wife was Queen Kaahumanu; she raised his son to become the next king. During the reign of Kamehameha the Great, the islands enjoyed long years of peace and stability. In 1778, white men arrived and brought livestock, fruits, and plants never before seen by the islanders. These foreigners also brought diseases and whiskey. Kamehameha accepted the foreigners and their innovations. He encouraged his people to accept

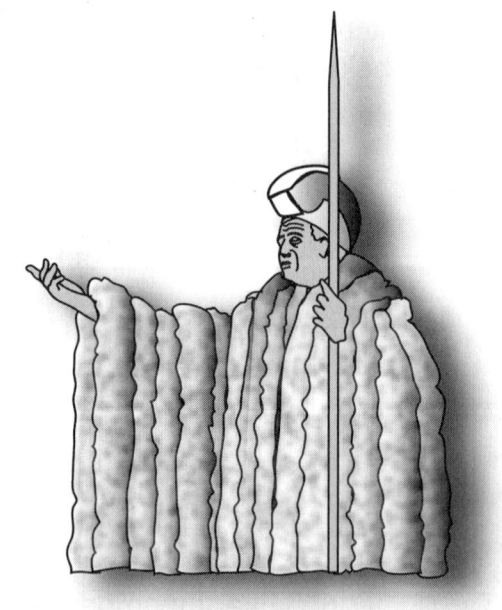

Every June 11, leis decorate Honolulu's statue of King Kamehameha I.

the white man's methods of agriculture and carpentry while retaining the old Hawaiian gods and customs. During his reign, Hawaii became an important center of trade.

Kamehameha I died in 1819 and was buried according to ancient customs. His bones were stripped of their flesh and hidden by his most trusted friends. The site of Kamehameha's burial remains unknown.

Upon Kamehameha's death, his son Liholiho, 22 years old, became King Kamehameha II, but it was widely believed that his strong-willed stepmother, Queen Kaahumanu, was the

© Mark Twain Media, Inc., Publishers

real power behind the throne. During Kamehameha II's reign (1819–1824), the first Christian missionaries arrived in Hawaii. They came to clothe the Hawaiians (who seldom wore clothes), to create a Hawaiian alphabet, and to bring the gospel to the natives. Unlike his father, Kamehameha I, Liholiho focused his attention on exploring the world outside of Hawaii. He was interested in how royals lived around the globe. With his favorite wife, six-foot-seven-inch Queen Kamamalu, and a large retinue, Liholiho traveled to London to visit the British queen. While there, Liholiho and members of his party contracted measles, for which Hawaiians had no immunity. Queen Kamamalu died. Heartbroken, Liholiho also died. Their bodies were returned to Hawaii for burial.

With the death of Kamehameha II, Liholiho's 10-year-old younger brother, Kauikeaouli, became King Kamehameha III and reigned from 1824 to 1854. Because the king was a child, Queen Kaahumanu served as Kamehameha III's regent until her death in 1832. She was a strong and cunning ruler. Under her influence, Kamehameha III became a Christian and banned traditional Hawaiian beliefs and practices, such as the hula. During his reign, citizens were given the right to vote for their representatives in government and were granted the right to religious freedom. Kauikeaouli made Hawaii a central trading post for the Pacific and increased Hawaii's recognition around the world. King Kamehameha III died in 1854.

King Kamehameha IV, Kauikeaouli's nephew Alexander, continued many of Kauikeaouli's programs. In order to prevent the annexation of Hawaii by the United States, Kamehameha IV developed diplomatic and trade relations with other countries. He also tried to slow the influence of Christian missionaries who continued to impact the Hawaiian people. Alexander and his wife Queen Emma had one son, Prince Albert—the last child ever born to a monarch of Hawaii. Albert died at the age of four of a brain fever. The king and queen were devastated by their son's death. At age 29, Alexander passed away. Some say it was out of grief over his son's death, but nefarious rumors said the king was poisoned.

When Alexander died, his older brother, Lot, became the king. Lot, who became Kamehameha V, reigned from 1863 to 1872, during which time Hawaii's influence and identity were expanded. Kamehameha V also restored some of the powers of the local chiefs. A stern, strong-willed man who weighed 375 pounds, King Kamehameha V seldom left his palace. The king resembled his great-grandfather, Kamehameha I, in appearance and temperament. When he died in 1872, the last of the Kamehameha kings was gone. From that point on, Hawaii's kings were elected.

King Kamehameha V (Lot) was the last of the Kamehameha kings.

Reading Engagement: Grade 8　　　　　　　　　　　Level Three, Lesson 1: American Royalty, Part I

Name: _____　Date: _____

Level Three, Lesson 1: American Royalty, Part I (cont.)

Reading Guide for "American Royalty, Part I"

BEFORE READING

Before reading "American Royalty, Part I," complete the **Before Reading** section of the Reading Guide.

A. Prereading Activity: Word Web

Word Web for Hawaii

Directions: Fill in the word web with information you know about Hawaii.

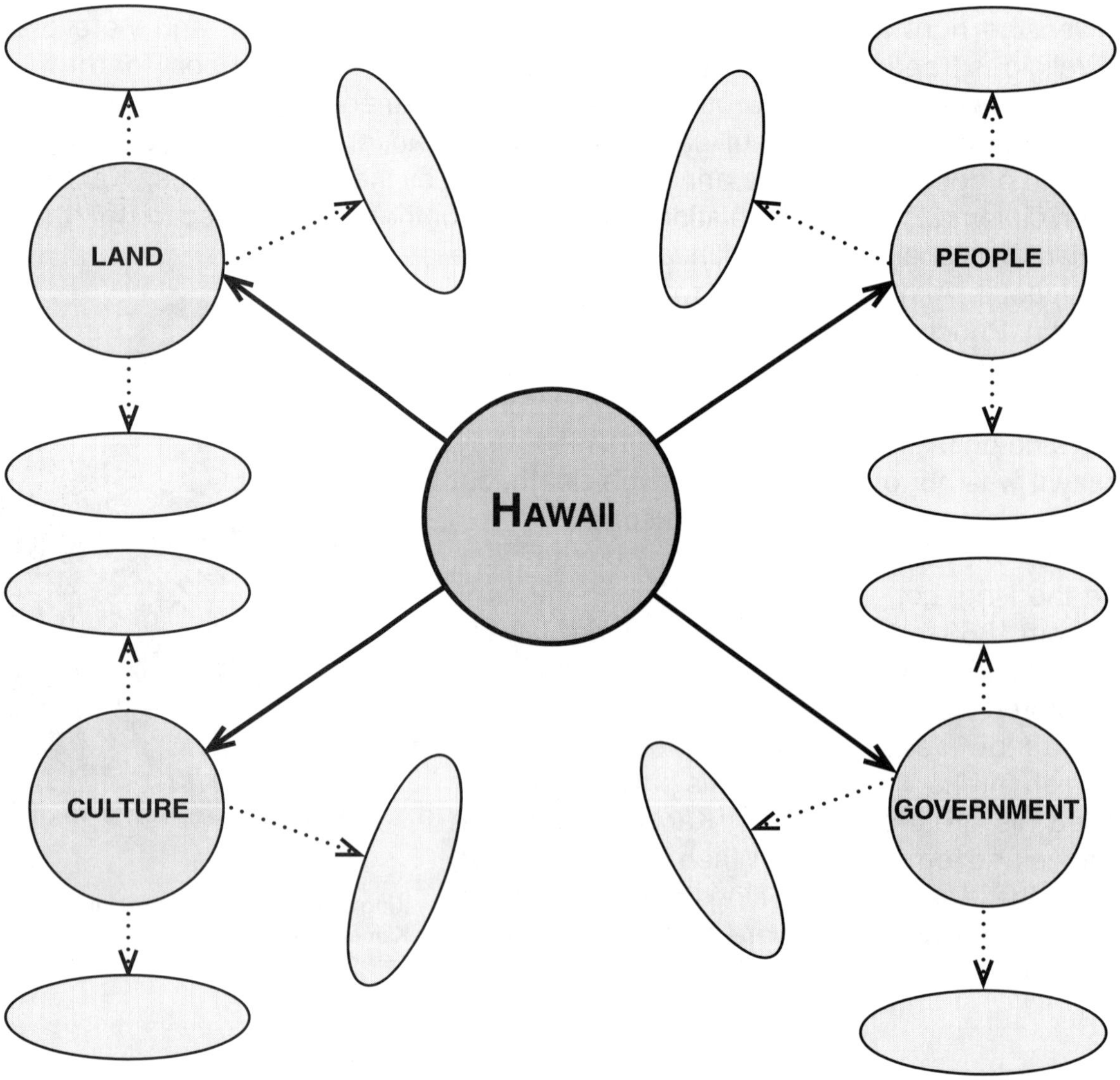

© Mark Twain Media, Inc., Publishers

Level Three, Lesson 1: American Royalty, Part I (cont.)

B. Vocabulary: Synonyms

What Does It Mean?

Directions: Read each word, and then choose another word (synonym) that means the same or nearly the same thing.

1. monarchy _____
2. unscrupulous _____
3. king _____
4. retinue _____
5. immunity _____
6. reigned _____
7. regent _____
8. cunning _____
9. nefarious _____
10. annexation _____

C. Prereading Questions

1. What do you think this reading is going to be about?

    _____

    _____

2. Read the questions in the **After Reading** section of this Reading Guide.

    a. Which question do you find the most interesting?

    _____

    _____

Reading Engagement: Grade 8   Level Three, Lesson 1: American Royalty, Part I

Name: _____ Date: _____

Level Three, Lesson 1: American Royalty, Part I (cont.)

b. Which answer do you think will be hardest to find?

_____

_____

3. What is your purpose for reading this story? Finish this sentence: I am reading to find out ...

_____

_____

DURING READING

1. Put a check mark in the margin next to the information that answers the questions in the **After Reading** section.

2. Circle any words you don't know when you come to them in the passage.

3. Put a question mark in the margin for anything you don't understand.

AFTER READING

1. READING THE LINES: Answer these questions by using information in the selection.

   a. Decide if each statement is true or false; circle the "T" if the statement is true and "F" if it is false.

   T F   1. Hawaii is the only state to have its own monarchy.

   T F   2. There are no royal palaces in the United States.

   T F   3. For over a hundred years, Hawaii was ruled by kings and queens.

   T F   4. Liliuokalani was the last Hawaiian royal.

   T F   5. Kamehameha means "the lovely one."

Level Three, Lesson 1: American Royalty, Part I (cont.)

    b.   How did King Kamehameha the Great come to power?

_____

_____

_____

    c.   Who was the "power behind the throne" for King Kamehameha II?

_____

_____

2.   READING BETWEEN THE LINES: Answer these questions by inferring ideas in the selection.

    a.   How did the Hawaiian monarchy lose its power?

_____

_____

_____

    b.   In what ways is the legend of King Kamehameha's birth similar to other stories and legends of the births of great leaders?

_____

_____

_____

_____

_____

    c.   What does the "power behind the throne" mean?

_____

_____

Reading Engagement: Grade 8   Level Three, Lesson 1: American Royalty, Part I

Name: _____ Date: _____

Level Three, Lesson 1: American Royalty, Part I (cont.)

    d.   What were the goals of the first Christian missionaries in Hawaii?

_____

_____

_____

3.   READING BEYOND THE LINES: Answer these questions with your own opinions.

    a.   Create a historical time line of the Hawaiian monarchy.

    b.   What were some of the causes of the demise of the Hawaiian monarchy?

_____

_____

_____

_____

ASSESSMENT/REINFORCEMENT

A.   Examine the Hawaiian Language Dictionary at www.traveltraveltravel.com/haw_language.htm to unlock the Hawaiian greeting at the top of this reading.

    What does the greeting say? _____

Level Three, Lesson 1: American Royalty, Part I (cont.)

B. Hawaiian Scramble: Solve each of the clues by unscrambling the words.

1. MHAKAEAMEH _____ was the name given to the first five kings of Hawaii.
2. The name Kamehameha means "the YNOELL _____ one."
3. During the reign of Kamehameha I, Hawaii became an ONTIMRTAP TCRENE _____ for trade.
4. NLIOALIULAIK _____ was the last of the royals to rule Hawaii.
5. HIIHOLOL _____ became Kamehameha II.
6. During Kamehameha II's reign, the first Christian SESRSMIIONAI _____ arrived to convert the natives.
7. Queen Kamamalu and Kamehameha II went to TEGRA NRITABI _____, where they contracted LAESEMS _____, and died.
8. After the death of Liholiho, his brother KULKUIEAOAI _____ became Kamehameha III.
9. During Kamehameha III's reign, Queen AUHKAMNUA _____ served as his regent until her death in 1832.
10. Queen Kaahumanu banned ALRADITIONT _____ Hawaiian beliefs and practices.
11. Kamehameha III's nephew NERALADEX _____ became Kamehameha IV.
12. Kamehameha IV developed MCLDOIPATI _____ and ERATD _____ relations with other countries to prevent the annexation of Hawaii by the United States.
13. He tried to slow the FUICENLEN _____ of Christian missionaries on the Hawaiian people.
14. Kamehameha IV and his wife, Queen Emma, had one son, CIRNEP RTLABE _____, who died of brain fever when he was four years old.
15. When Alexander died, his older brother, Lot, became King Kamehameha V. He restored some of the powers of the COLAL IFCSHE _____.

Reading Engagement: Grade 8   Level Three, Lesson 2: The Day the Music Died

Name: _____ Date: _____

Level Three, Lesson 2: The Day the Music Died

The Day the Music Died

February 3, 1959, Clear Lake, Iowa—Following an appearance before a thousand adoring fans, rock 'n roll icons Buddy Holly, Ritchie Valens, and J.P. Richardson (also known as the Big Bopper) died when their four-seat single engine plane crashed minutes after takeoff. The loss of these three musicians, especially Buddy Holly, was enormous. Singer/songwriter Don McLean in his hit song, "American Pie," called it "the day the music died."

Holly, one of the founding fathers of rock 'n roll, is widely considered its single most influential and creative force. Buddy Holly was a pioneer and innovator. He played guitar and sang, composed songs, and arranged unique recordings of these songs. In his brief 18-month career, Buddy Holly produced a body of work that is considered some of the best in rock 'n roll history. His music influenced not only recording contemporaries but marked the future direction music would take.

Buddy Holly was born Charles Harden Holley—a name his mother said was too big for such a small boy. Nicknamed Buddy, Holly was the youngest of four children in a very musical family; his mother played the piano and sang, his brother Larry played the fiddle, Buddy played the guitar, and brother Travis played the accordion. His sister Pat played the piano and sang. The Holley family was supportive, honest, religious, and hard-working.

As a child, Buddy showed a quick aptitude for music and was able to play complicated songs by ear. He studied piano, violin, and steel guitar but loved the acoustic guitar the best. Though his musical training was brief, it was eclectic: blues, country-western, rhythm and blues, and gospel. His early influences were Hank Williams and Jimmy Rodgers.

By junior high school, Buddy was accomplished on guitar, banjo, and mandolin. With a friend (Bob Montgomery), he formed a duo, "Buddy and Bob," and played at school functions, in talent shows, at car dealerships, grand openings, and promotion parties. Bob Montgomery sang the lead and was principal composer. As the duo got older, they played local radio shows, high school dances, and youth clubs and centers in New Mexico and Texas. Their first "professional" gig was a half-hour radio program Sunday nights on KDAV, an all-country radio station. Gradually the lead switched to Buddy, who sang more "western bop."

In high school, the group called themselves The Crickets, and Holly sang vocals and played lead guitar, Jerry Allison played the drums, Joe Mauldin played bass, and Niki Sullivan played rhythm guitar. At times Larry Welborn played bass, and Sonny Curtis played guitar. The group made their own demo records and sent them to record companies hoping for a recording contract.

© Mark Twain Media, Inc., Publishers

Level Three, Lesson 2: The Day the Music Died (cont.)

Buddy Holly and The Crickets were not an overnight success, but they were in the right place at the right time. Radio station KDAV sponsored rock 'n roll concerts and chose Buddy, Bob, and The Crickets to open shows for performers Marty Robbins, Porter Wagoner, and Elvis Presley. Holly was very impressed with Elvis and later said, "Without Elvis Presley, none of us would have made it." Eventually a record producer heard Buddy and Bob and signed Holly to a recording contract with Decca Records. However, his attempt to break into the rock 'n roll charts was a colossal failure ... at the time.

Buddy Holly (he dropped the "e" in Holley) and his group, The Crickets, recorded "That'll Be The Day" in June of 1957. The song was a hit, and the group went on an 80-day tour with other performers like Fats Domino and the Everly Brothers. By December of 1957 Holly had two other songs in the top forty: "Oh, Boy!" and "Peggy Sue." The group made their first guest appearance on "The Ed Sullivan Show" and subsequently joined rockers Paul Anka and Jerry Lee Lewis for a short Australian tour.

Holly's 25-day tour of England was a huge success, and music critics see this as pivotal in popular music. In the audience were Paul McCartney and John Lennon before they were famous. Holly greatly influenced McCartney and Lennon and their group in name, dress, songs, and music production. McCartney and Lennon got the idea for the name of their band, The Beatles, from Holly's Crickets. Unlike other rock 'n roll groups at the time, Holly dressed in a shirt, tie, and jacket; the Beatles copied his manner of dress and type of music. Holly popularized the rock-band formula: 2 guitars, bass, and drums; McCartney and Lennon played guitar, Harrison played bass, and Ringo Starr played the drums.

1958 was an eventful year for Holly. He fell in love with and married Maria Elena Santiago in August, and then split with The Crickets in the fall because he was tired of touring; he wanted to settle down with Maria in New York. However, he had major financial difficulties due to the monstrous mismanagement of his money by his manager. In January, he decided to do a three-week tour through the frozen Midwest to make some quick money.

The "Winter Dance Party Tour" starred 22-year-old Buddy Holly, 17-year-old Mexican-American Ritchie Valens, whose song, "Donna" was number 1 in America, and 27-year-old J.P. Richardson, "The Big Bopper," whose song, "Chantilly Lace" was in the top ten. The tour was plagued with problems from the start. The freezing weather resulted in colds and flu among the performers, and the buses were poorly heated and kept breaking down. Following a show in Clear Lake, Iowa, Holly chartered a small plane for himself and band members Tommy Alsup and Waylon Jennings. At the last minute, Alsup gave up his seat to Valens who had never ridden in a small plane and kept pestering Alsup to let him go in his place. Jennings gave up his seat to Richardson, who had the flu. At 1:00 A.M. the plane took off into a furious snowstorm. Five minutes later, the pilot, blinded by the weather, flew the plane into the ground, killing all on board.

The news of the crash was devastating to teens everywhere. Singer/songwriter Don McLean remembered the rock 'n rollers in his song, "American Pie":

"I can't remember if I cried
When I read about his widowed bride
But something touched me deep inside
The day the music died."

Buddy Holly had an enormous influence on popular music. His spirit, creativity, extraordinary ingenuity, his high level of engineering, and his willingness to experiment set him apart from the musicians of his time. His style of guitar playing has been copied by every rock group since 1958. Sonny Curtis, a friend of Holly's, said it best, "Buddy Holly lives whenever rock 'n roll is played."

Ritchie Valens

Buddy Holly

J.P. Richardson, "The Big Bopper"

Reading Engagement: Grade 8 　　　　　　　　　　Level Three, Lesson 2: The Day the Music Died

Name: _____ Date: _____

Level Three, Lesson 2: The Day the Music Died (cont.)

Reading Guide for "The Day the Music Died"

BEFORE READING

Before reading "The Day the Music Died," complete the **Before Reading** section of the Reading Guide.

A. Prereading Activity

**Rock 'n Roll
What Do Ya Know?**

Directions: See how many of these rock 'n roll trivia questions you can answer.

1. Who is known as the King of Rock 'n Roll?

   _____

2. Who was "The Big Bopper"?

   _____

3. What was the name of Buddy Holly's band?

   _____

4. What band was the greatest rock 'n roll band of all time?

   _____

5. When did rock 'n roll begin to gain enormous popularity?

   _____

Reading Engagement: Grade 8   Level Three, Lesson 2: The Day the Music Died

Name: _____ Date: _____

Level Three, Lesson 2: The Day the Music Died (cont.)

B. Vocabulary: Definitions

What Is It?

Directions: What do the vocabulary words mean? If you don't know, use a dictionary.

<u>These words describe Buddy Holly or his music.</u>

1. icon _____
2. innovator _____
3. unique _____
4. eclectic _____
5. ingenuity _____

<u>These words are musical instruments.</u>

6. accordion _____
7. acoustic guitar _____
8. mandolin _____

<u>These words are also in the reading.</u>

9. pivotal _____
10. plagued _____
11. gig _____
12. colossal _____

C. Prereading Questions

1. What do you think this reading is going to be about?

   _____

   _____

Level Three, Lesson 2: The Day the Music Died (cont.)

2. Read the questions in the **After Reading** section of this Reading Guide.

   a. Which question do you find the most interesting?

   _____

   _____

   b. Which answer do you think will be hardest to find?

   _____

   _____

3. What is your purpose for reading this story? Finish this sentence: I am reading to find out ...

   _____

   _____

DURING READING

1. Put a check mark in the margin next to the information that answers the questions in the **After Reading** section.

2. Circle any words you don't know when you come to them in the passage.

3. Put a question mark in the margin for anything you don't understand.

AFTER READING

1. READING THE LINES: Answer these questions by using information in the selection.

   a. What was "the day the music died"?

   _____

   _____

   _____

   b. What were some of Holly's accomplishments?

   _____

   _____

Level Three, Lesson 2: The Day the Music Died (cont.)

c. How old were the three musicians when they died?

_____

_____

d. How did Charles Harden Holley become Buddy Holly?

_____

_____

_____

e. Who were Paul McCartney and John Lennon?

_____

_____

_____

2. READING BETWEEN THE LINES: Answer these questions by inferring ideas in the selection.

a. What is the difference between a steel guitar, an acoustic guitar, and a rhythm guitar?

_____

_____

_____

b. Who were some of the stars and what was some of the music that influenced Buddy Holly?

_____

_____

Reading Engagement: Grade 8   Level Three, Lesson 2: The Day the Music Died

Name: _____ Date: _____

Level Three, Lesson 2: The Day the Music Died (cont.)

    c. What did Buddy Holly mean when he said, "Without Elvis Presley, none of us would have made it."?

_____

_____

_____

    d. What were some of the problems Holly faced in 1958?

_____

_____

_____

3. READING BEYOND THE LINES: Answer these questions with your own opinions.

    a. Why did singer Don McLean see the plane crash as "the day the music died"?

_____

_____

_____

    b. Who is the "widowed bride" in the lyrics to "American Pie"?

_____

_____

    c. It is always sad when people die young and in their prime. Who are some other public figures who have also died young?

_____

_____

_____

Reading Engagement: Grade 8   Level Three, Lesson 2: The Day the Music Died

Name: _____ Date: _____

Level Three, Lesson 2: The Day the Music Died (cont.)

ASSESSMENT/REINFORCEMENT

A. Listen to any one or more of these Buddy Holly hit songs. What is your opinion of his work?

- "That'll Be the Day" – 1957
- "Peggy Sue" – 1957
- "Everyday" – 1957
- "Oh Boy!" – 1957
- "Not Fade Away" – 1957
- "Maybe Baby" – 1958
- "Rave On" – 1958
- "Heartbeat" – 1958
- "Well All Right" – 1958

Level Three, Lesson 2: The Day the Music Died (cont.)

B. Label the following instruments with their correct names from the word bank. Buddy Holly played many of these instruments in his lifetime.

WORD BANK

| accordion | acoustic guitar | banjo | bass guitar |
| mandolin | rhythm guitar | steel guitar | violin |

1. _____

2. _____

3. _____

4. _____

5. _____

6. _____

7. _____

8. _____

Level Three, Lesson 3: "Mr. Television"

"Mr. Television"

Milton Berle was an enormously popular American comedian who performed in vaudeville, radio, silent movies, television, and film. He was also an accomplished songwriter and author of three books. His best-known work was in television in the late 1940s and early 1950s where he was affectionately known as "Mr. Television." Milton Berle was actually the first person to appear on television in an experimental broadcast in New York City in 1928.

Born in a five-story walkup in New York City on July 12, 1908, Milton Berle began life as Mendel Berlinger. He began his career at the age of 5 by winning a contest for Charlie Chaplin imitators. Pushed by his mother, a true stage mother, Berle went on to become a highly respected child actor of "flickers," appearing in more than 50 silent movies. In 1916, he was enrolled in the New York Professional Children's School. At the age of 12, he made his stage debut in Atlantic City and spent the next decade in vaudeville. He also made his way up through the vaudeville circuit honing his persona as a brash comic known for stealing the material of fellow comedians. Berle himself had one of the largest joke collections in the world with about 6.5 million jokes on his computer. Berle made his film debut as an adult in 1937 and starred in a number of Hollywood films as a brash, wisecracking character. He continued to polish his comedy routines in nightclubs and on the radio.

Milton Berle gained national recognition and popularity when he entered television in 1948. He starred as the host of Texaco Star Theater, an hour-long variety show that included slapstick vaudeville routines, music, and comedy sketches. The show became so popular that people didn't go out of their houses on Tuesday nights at 8 o'clock because Milton Berle was on. Nightclubs changed their closing from Monday nights to Tuesday nights because of the popularity of Berle's show. Restaurants were empty for the hour he was on the air, and attendance at movies and theaters plummeted. *Life* magazine reported that in 1947 there were 17 television stations in the United States broadcasting to 136,000 television sets. As a consequence of "Mr. Television's" success, by the end of 1948 there were more than 50 stations broadcasting to more than 700,000 television sets.

Within two months of the show's broadcast, Berle became the first television superstar with the highest ratings ever attained. Arguably the most famous man in America during those years (1948–1954), Milton Berle was soon referred to as "Mr. Television," "Mr. Tuesday Night," and "Uncle Miltie." For an audience used to radio, the addition of the visual medium was enthusiastically applauded. In 1951, his contract with NBC granted him $200,000 a year for 30 years if he appeared exclusively for NBC. His show was also one of the first television shows to promote merchandising, including Uncle Miltie T-shirts, comic books, and chewing gum.

Uncle Miltie opened each weekly show in some sort of outrageous costume, and the show continued with visual vaudeville routines, music, comedy sketches, and singing. Berle was constantly interjecting himself in the acts of his guests; his use of sight gags, props, and visual style was well-suited for television. "I think laughter is very imperative. And that's the important part of my life, of making people laugh so they can forget their problems," Berle once said. "A good laugh is better than anything." The show changed its name and its sponsor in 1953 and became "The Milton Berle Show." The show's popularity began to dissipate in the 1960s with the convergence of a more sophisticated television audience and better TV programming. Audiences were tired of Berle's manic energy and wild shenanigans, and the show eventually was cancelled.

Following the show's demise, Milton Berle was unable to find new television work, so he made nightclub appearances, appeared on Broadway, played Las Vegas, appeared in many films, and was often a guest on other people's variety shows. A frequent performer at charity benefits, Berle was a popular host of celebrity roasts in his later years. He wrote and published over 400 songs and wrote three books.

Berle won an Emmy award in 1949 and was given a lifetime achievement award in 1979. He was one of the first seven inductees into the Television Academy Hall of Fame in 1984. In 1991, he became the first entertainer inducted into the International Comedy Hall of Fame. He was one of the first members of the Academy of Television Arts and Sciences Hall of Fame and president of the Friars Club for more than a decade. Milton Berle also received the Yiddish Theatrical Alliance Humanitarian Award in 1951, the *Look* Magazine TV Award, and was the National Academy of Arts and Sciences Man of the Year in 1959.

Milton Berle died of colon cancer at his Los Angeles home on March 27, 2002, at the age of 93. In a written statement released at the time, Bob Hope eulogized Berle, "What a remarkable man, what a remarkable career. Eighty-eight years in show business, a brilliant comedian, an accomplished actor, a lifelong friend." In his own words, Berle said,

> "I'd rather be a could-be if I cannot be an are;
> because a could-be is a maybe who is reaching for a star.
> I'd rather be a has-been than a might-have-been, by far;
> for a might-have-been has never been,
> but a has was once an are."

Reading Engagement: Grade 8   Level Three, Lesson 3: "Mr. Television"

Name: _____   Date: _____

Level Three, Lesson 3: "Mr. Television" (cont.)

Reading Guide for "Mr. Television"

BEFORE READING

Before reading "Mr. Television," complete the **Before Reading** section of the Reading Guide.

A. Prereading Activity: Activating Background Knowledge

Television Word Search

Directions: Find and circle the hidden words within the grid of letters. Words may be printed forward, backward, horizontally, vertically, or diagonally. When you are finished, write the first 24 uncircled letters in the puzzle (when reading from left to right) on the blanks below the puzzle to find the hidden message.

Lucille Ball

The Lone Ranger with his horse, Silver

Ed Sullivan

___ ___ ___ ___ ___ ___ ___ ___ ___ ___ ___ ___   ___ ___ ___

___ ___ ___   ___ ___ ___ ___ ___ ___ ___ ___ ___

Davy Crockett	I Love Lucy	Perry Como	Your Hit Parade
Ed Sullivan	Lone Ranger	Today	What's My Line
Father Knows Best	People are Funny		

© Mark Twain Media, Inc., Publishers

Reading Engagement: Grade 8 | Level Three, Lesson 3: "Mr. Television"

Name: _____ Date: _____

Level Three, Lesson 3: "Mr. Television" (cont.)

B. Vocabulary

"Mr. Television" Vocabulary

Directions: Write the pronunciation of each of these words.

1. persona _____
2. plummeted _____
3. eulogized _____
4. vaudeville _____
5. merchandising _____
6. imperative _____
7. dissipate _____
8. demise _____

C. Prereading Questions

1. What do you think this reading is going to be about?

   _____

   _____

2. Read the questions in the **After Reading** section of this Reading Guide.

   a. Which question do you find the most interesting?

   _____

   _____

   b. Which answer do you think will be hardest to find?

   _____

   _____

Reading Engagement: Grade 8

Name: _____ Date: _____

Level Three, Lesson 3: "Mr. Television" (cont.)

3. What is your purpose for reading this story? Finish this sentence: I am reading to find out ...

_____

_____

DURING READING

1. Put a check mark in the margin next to the information that answers the questions in the **After Reading** section.

2. Circle any words you don't know when you come to them in the passage.

3. Put a question mark in the margin for anything you don't understand.

AFTER READING

1. READING THE LINES: Answer these questions by using information in the selection.

   a. What is another name for "flickers"?

   _____

   b. How did Milton Berle gain national recognition?

   _____

   _____

   _____

   c. What are some of Milton Berle's nicknames?

   _____

   _____

   _____

Reading Engagement: Grade 8   Level Three, Lesson 3: "Mr. Television"

Name: _____ Date: _____

Level Three, Lesson 3: "Mr. Television" (cont.)

d. Why did NBC cancel "The Milton Berle Show"?

_____

_____

2. READING BETWEEN THE LINES: Answer these questions by inferring ideas in the selection.

a. What is a five-story walkup?

_____

_____

_____

b. What does "honing his persona" mean?

_____

_____

_____

c. What is a stage mother?

_____

_____

_____

d. What is a synonym for *shenanigans*?

_____

Level Three, Lesson 3: "Mr. Television" (cont.)

3. READING BEYOND THE LINES: Answer these questions with your own opinions.

   a. What was Berle saying about himself through the poem?

   _____

   _____

   _____

   _____

   b. From what you've read, did Berle live up to his nicknames? Why or why not?

   _____

   _____

   _____

   c. How did Berle's show impact the nation?

   _____

   _____

   _____

   _____

ASSESSMENT/REINFORCEMENT

A. The following shows were popular during the "golden age of television." Research any one of them so you can describe it to your classmates. Perhaps your class could do a thematic unit on the "golden age of television."

Davy Crockett	I Love Lucy	Perry Como	Your Hit Parade
Ed Sullivan	Lone Ranger	Today	What's My Line?
Father Knows Best	People are Funny		

Reading Engagement: Grade 8   Level Three, Lesson 3: "Mr. Television"

Name: _____ Date: _____

Level Three, Lesson 3: "Mr. Television" (cont.)

B. Vaudeville Matching: Before television there was vaudeville. Vaudeville was a stage show consisting of specialty acts, including songs, dance, comic skits, and acrobatic performances. Milton Berle performed in vaudeville for many years. Below is a list of vaudeville slang. Match each definition in the second column with its corresponding term in the first column by placing the letter on the blank next to the term. Use the Internet or other reference sources if you need help.

_____ 1. Playing to the haircuts
_____ 2. Deuce spot
_____ 3. Combination house
_____ 4. Death Trail
_____ 5. Snake
_____ 6. Gagging
_____ 7. Guttenburg
_____ 8. Hand-to-hand music
_____ 9. Hokum or hocum
_____ 10. Knocked 'em bowlegged
_____ 11. Papering the house
_____ 12. Build up
_____ 13. Relatives in the ice business
_____ 14. Chooser
_____ 15. Fish

A. Wardrobe
B. Giving away free tickets to fill up the audience; often done on opening night or when a critic is in the audience. This practice is still in use.
C. A lousy act
D. Contortionist
E. Last on the bill; in other words, playing to the backs of the audiences as they left the theater
F. What an unresponsive audience must have
G. A theater showing both motion pictures and vaudeville
H. Bits, jokes, and routines that were corny, old-fashioned, and contrived
I. To introduce a number in order to interest the audience and prepare them to fully appreciate it
J. Applause
K. A performer who goes to see other acts to steal material
L. Was a big success
M. The second on the bill; considered to be the worst spot in the program
N. Introducing unplanned and unrehearsed remarks, reactions, bits, or business into an act during a performance; used to draw focus or to throw off the other performer(s)
O. A string of small, cheap theaters extending from Chicago to the Northwest, down the Pacific Coast, to finish up in Southern California

Level Three, Lesson 4: Happy New Year!

Happy New Year!

New Year's Day is probably the oldest and most universally celebrated holiday in the world. It is a day for both secular and religious celebrations rich in tradition. These rituals symbolically abolish the past and welcome the new year. January 1st, in some countries, is considered "Everyman's Birthday," and on this day, every citizen becomes one year older. It is also the day the earth begins another orbit of the sun during which it will travel 583,416,000 miles in 365.2422 days. New Year's Day is a time of rejuvenation, resolutions, and relaxation, and a time for family, friends, and feasting.

January 1st hasn't always been New Year's Day. Four thousand years ago, the ancient Babylonians celebrated the New Year with the beginning of spring. Their New Year holiday lasted eleven days. In 46 B.C., Julius Caesar established a new calendar in which he changed New Year's Day to January 1st for political reasons. It was the day after the Roman elections and the day upon which the newly elected senators assumed their new positions. (It was also the day of the first new moon in January.) In A.D. 567 the Council of Tours changed the date of the new year to the day of the vernal equinox (around March 25th). This New Year's celebration lasted for several days. When the Gregorian calendar (the one most of the world uses now) was adopted, the New Year was once again January 1st, and it has so remained since then.

Religious, cultural, and social observances of the New Year are not always on January 1st. The Jewish New Year, Rosh Hashanah, is on the first and second days of Tishri, which is sometimes in September or early October. Rosh Hashanah is a time for rejoicing as well as a time for serious introspection; it is a time to take stock of one's life. On the Islamic calendar, the New Year begins on the first day of spring (21 March). For New Year's Day, Muslims clean their houses, buy new clothes, and set a special table with seven articles that all must begin with the letter "s" for **Haft-sin**: sonbul (hyacinth), sabzeh (green shoots grown from grain), samanoo (a sweet pudding made of green wheat), serkeh (vinegar), sumac (an herb), seeb (an apple), and senjed (bohemian olives). Also on the table are a bowl of colored eggs, candles, a mirror, a bowl of rose water, and a copy of the Koran. Everyone gathers around the New Year table for a special feast. In Iran (formerly Persia) today, gifts are often exchanged. The Hindu New Year is called Diwali and is celebrated for three days in late October or early November. **Diwali** is a festival of lights and a time for new beginnings. Hindus give cards and gifts; they make New Year's resolutions and forget quarrels, for Diwali is a time to be happy and generous. Some Christian denominations celebrate the New Year with the Feast of Christ's Circumcision. However, many Christians focus on the birth of Christ, celebrated on December 25, and the resurrection of Christ, which is celebrated at Easter.

Level Three, Lesson 4: Happy New Year! (cont.)

Not all countries celebrate New Year's at the same time or in the same way. The Chinese celebrate New Year's sometime between January 10th and February 19th, at the time of the new moon. At Chinese New Year, called **Yuan Tan**, people wear red clothes, decorate with poems on red paper, and give children "lucky money" in red envelopes. (Red is considered a lucky color.) The biggest and most exciting part of Chinese New Year is the Festival of Lanterns, a giant street procession with thousands of lanterns used to light the way for the New Year. The Chinese believe there may be evil spirits around at New Year, so they set off firecrackers to frighten the spirits away.

The Japanese New Year is called **Oshogatsu**; it begins on January 1st and lasts for two weeks. It is a time for family celebrations, for laughter, and for good luck. Two festivals mark the Japanese New Year: the Greater and the Lesser. The Greater Festival includes prayers that are offered for the dead, and friends exchange gifts and visits. The Lesser Festival includes prayers for good crops and offerings to the god of the rice paddy. An elaborate bird-scaring ritual also takes place. The Japanese also believe evil spirits may be lurking around, so they hang a rope of straw across the front of their homes; this represents happiness and good luck. At midnight on New Year's Eve, the Japanese begin to laugh; this is supposed to bring good luck in the new year.

Cung-Chuc Tan-Xuan is "Happy New Year" in Vietnamese. In Vietnam, New Year is called **Tet Nguyen Dan** (or **Tet** for short), which means the first morning of the first day of the new year. It falls between the harvesting of the crops and the sowing of the new crops—sometime between January 21 and February 19—and lasts for seven days. The Vietnamese believe there is a god in every home, and at the New Year, this god travels to heaven where he or she will say how good or bad each member of the family has been in the past year.

The New Year in the West is both universal and unique. Australians celebrate the New Year on January 1st. It is a day for outdoor activities like rodeos, picnics, races, and surf carnivals. Many Australians camp out on the beach on New Year's Eve. At midnight, they ring in the New Year by making noise with whistles, rattles, car horns, and church bells. In Russia, Grandfather Frost (similar to our Santa Claus) arrives on New Year's Eve with his bag of toys. He wears blue instead of red and can punish any evildoer by freezing him or her. Children dance around the New Year's tree and tell rhymes to Father Frost before receiving their presents. In Greece, New Year's Day is also the Festival of St. Basil, who was famous for his kindness. Children leave their shoes by the fire on New Year's Day with the hope that St. Basil will come and fill their shoes with gifts. In Scotland, New Year's is called **Hogmanay**. Scottish people believe that the first person to enter your house in the New Year will bring good or bad luck; it is very good luck if the first visitor to your house is a tall, dark-haired man bringing gifts. In some towns in

Scotland, barrels of tar are set on fire and rolled through the streets. This signifies that the old year is burned up, and the new one is allowed to enter. The song, "Auld Lang Syne" is sung at midnight on New Year's Eve.

Typical New Year's activities in the United States are parties, dances, parades, and football. Watching football games on New Year's Day is a tradition that was begun in 1902. The annual Tournament of Roses Parade began in 1886 with members of the Valley Hunt Club decorating their carriages with flowers to celebrate the ripening of the orange crop in California. On New Year's Eve people gather in Times Square in New York to watch the lowering of a giant crystal ball. At the stroke of midnight, people sing "Auld Lang Syne" and kiss their sweethearts.

The New Year is celebrated at different times and in different ways by people around the world. In one way or another, people celebrate the passing of the "old" year and the coming of the "new" year with friends, family, and festivities.

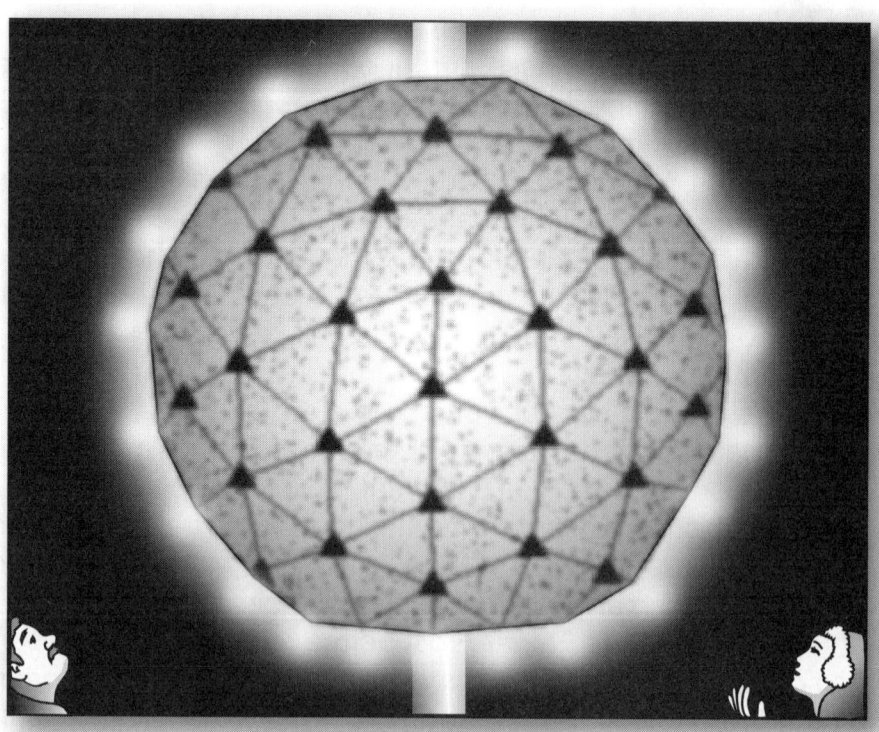

Level Three, Lesson 4: Happy New Year! (cont.)

Reading Guide for "Happy New Year!"

BEFORE READING

Before reading "Happy New Year!", complete the **Before Reading** section of the Reading Guide.

A. Prereading Activity: Activating Background Knowledge

New Year Traditions

Directions: How is New Year's celebrated in your family? Is it a religious or a social holiday? What are some of the traditions of your family? Does your family eat special food on this holiday? Write a paragraph describing how the New Year is celebrated at your house.

_____

_____

_____

_____

_____

_____

_____

_____

_____

_____

Reading Engagement: Grade 8   Level Three, Lesson 4: Happy New Year!

Level Three, Lesson 4: Happy New Year! (cont.)

B. **Vocabulary: Alliteration**

New Year Vocabulary

Directions: Alliteration is a literary term that means the reiteration of an initial consonant. The words below are examples of alliteration found in this reading. In each box, choose the correct word for each sentence.

      rejuvenation   **resolution**   **relaxation**

1. This New Year's I made a _____ to put more _____ in my schedule, and I feel an overwhelming sense of _____.

      family   **friends**   **feasting**

2. My _____ were _____ on my birthday with my _____.

      holy day   **holiday**

3. Halloween is a _____, but All Souls' Day is a _____.

      universal   **unique**

4. How we celebrate the New Year is _____, but the fact that we all celebrate the New Year is _____.

© Mark Twain Media, Inc., Publishers

Reading Engagement: Grade 8   Level Three, Lesson 4: Happy New Year!

Name: _____ Date: _____

Level Three, Lesson 4: Happy New Year! (cont.)

C. Prereading Questions

1. What do you think this reading is going to be about?

   _____

   _____

2. Read the questions in the **After Reading** section of this Reading Guide.

   a. Which question do you find the most interesting?

   _____

   _____

   b. Which answer do you think will be hardest to find?

   _____

   _____

3. What is your purpose for reading this story? Finish this sentence: I am reading to find out ...

   _____

   _____

DURING READING

1. Put a check mark in the margin next to the information that answers the questions in the **After Reading** section.

2. Circle any words you don't know when you come to them in the passage.

3. Put a question mark in the margin for anything you don't understand.

Level Three, Lesson 4: Happy New Year! (cont.)

AFTER READING

1. READING THE LINES: Answer these questions by using information in the selection.

   a. New Year's hasn't always been on January 1st. Name some of the other days on which this holiday occurred.

   _____
   _____
   _____

   b. What is Rosh Hashanah, and why is it an important day for Jews?

   _____
   _____
   _____

   c. How do the Japanese bring good luck on New Year's Eve?

   _____
   _____

   d. What are the names of at least three religious New Year's holidays?

   _____
   _____

2. READING BETWEEN THE LINES: Answer these questions by inferring ideas in the selection.

   a. Why did the Romans change New Year's on the Julian calendar?

   _____
   _____

Level Three, Lesson 4: Happy New Year! (cont.)

b. Name a religious New Year's activity.

_____

Name a cultural New Year's activity.

_____

Name a social New Year's activity.

_____

c. What is the name of the New Year holiday for each of these, and when is the holiday celebrated?

Religion/Country	Name of Holiday	When Celebrated
1. Christian		
2. Muslim		
3. Jewish		
4. Hindu		
5. Chinese		
6. Japanese		
7. Vietnamese		
8. Australian		
9. Russian		
10. Greek		
11. Scottish		

Level Three, Lesson 4: Happy New Year! (cont.)

3. READING BEYOND THE LINES: Answer these questions with your own opinions.

    a. Do you think celebrating "Everyman's Birthday" is a good idea? Why or why not?

    _____
    _____
    _____
    _____

    b. In your opinion, when should the new year begin? Why?

    _____
    _____
    _____
    _____

    c. In your opinion, which is the most interesting New Year's tradition? Why?

    _____
    _____
    _____
    _____

ASSESSMENT/REINFORCEMENT

A. What are the words to the song, "Auld Lang Syne"? Research on the Internet or in other resources to find out. Why do people in the English-speaking world sing this song at midnight on New Year's Eve?

_____
_____
_____
_____

B. **New Year's Criss-Cross Puzzle:** Use a pencil for this puzzle. Using the boldface words in the sentences on the next page, fit them into the puzzle. Two words may fit in the same boxes, but if you are unable to connect the next word, you know you have written in the wrong word. Erase and continue with another word that fits. The first words have been done for you. To continue, find a six-letter word whose last letter is an "r."

Level Three, Lesson 4: Happy New Year! (cont.)

    The celebration of the **new year** is the oldest of all holidays. It was first observed in ancient **Babylon** about 4,000 years ago with the celebration lasting eleven days. In the years around 2000 B.C., the Babylonian New Year began with the first **new moon**. The making of New Year's **resolutions** also dates back to the early Babylonians, with the returning of borrowed **farm equipment** at the top of the resolution list.

    The tradition of using a **baby** to signify the new year was begun in Greece around 600 B.C. It was their **tradition** at that time to parade a baby in a basket to symbolize **annual rebirth**. Early **Egyptians** also used a baby as a symbol of rebirth. The image of a baby with a New Year's **banner** as a symbolic representation of the New Year was brought to early America by the **Germans**. They had used this image since the 14th century.

    Some traditional new year foods are thought to bring luck. Many cultures believe that anything in the shape of a **ring** is good luck because it symbolizes "coming **full circle**," or completing a year's cycle. For that reason, the Dutch believe that eating **donuts** on New Year's Day will bring good fortune. People in many parts of the United States celebrate the new year by consuming **black-eyed peas**. These legumes are typically accompanied by either hog jowls or ham. Black-eyed peas and other **legumes** are considered good luck in many cultures. The hog is considered lucky because it symbolizes **prosperity**. Cabbage is another good-luck **vegetable** that is eaten on New Year's Day by many. **Cabbage leaves** are considered a sign of prosperity because they represent currency. In some regions, **rice** is a lucky food eaten on New Year's Day.

Level Four, Lesson 1: American Royalty, Part II

American Royalty, Part II

For nearly a hundred years, from the reign of the first royal, King Kamehameha the Great, to the reign of the last royal, Queen Liliuokalani, the royal families ruled the hearts and minds of the Hawaiian people through the Hawaiian temples and chiefs. The monarchy was replaced by a constitutional monarchy during the reign of King Kalakaua; the constitutional monarchy was replaced in 1894 by an American-style government brought about by a coup.

Upon the death of King Kamehameha V in 1872, Lunalilo, the half-brother of the king, was chosen as the next king of Hawaii by the Hawaiian Legislature. The new king never married, although he was engaged for a while, and did not have any children. King Lunalilo had many foreign advisors, but he also had a true concern for his people. Lunalilo died within a year of becoming king, leaving his estate to needy Hawaiians. Some believe Lunalilo was poisoned because of his concern for the Hawaiian people.

Once again the Hawaiian legislature met to choose a new king. They chose David Kalakaua, a chief of royal blood who was descended from Kamehameha the Great. King Kalakaua was well-educated, intelligent, and at ease equally with foreigners and Hawaiians alike. During Kalakaua's reign, 1874–1891, a group of foreign traders and businessmen formed a militia group and forced the king to accept a new constitutional amendment that stripped the monarchy of all power, making the king a figurehead only. This amendment permitted white foreigners to vote in elections, though it denied that right to Japanese, Chinese, and other Asian residents of Hawaii. King David Kalakaua died of kidney disease while on a trip to San Francisco.

Queen Liliuokalani was the last Hawaiian monarch.

The last Hawaiian monarch, Queen Liliuokalani, a brilliant and talented woman, was sister to David Kalakaua. As a child, she loved horseback riding, tea parties, and singing. As an adult, Liliuokalani composed music and was a published songwriter. She composed over 100 songs, including the famous "Aloha Oe." Liliuokalani was also a courageous and intelligent woman, but her many troubles began almost immediately after she became queen. She tried valiantly to regain the power surrendered to the Hawaiian Legislature by her brother, King Kalakaua. As a strong nationalist, Liliuokalani tried unsuccessfully to replace the old constitution with one that would favor native Hawaiians.

In January of 1893, the U.S. minister, John L. Stevens, conspired with other non-Hawaiians to overthrow the monarchy and establish a republican form of government with the goal of annexation by the United States. Armed troops were sent ashore from a United States warship in Honolulu Harbor, and Liliuokalani was forced to surrender her throne to a provisional government. In 1894, the Republic of Hawaii was established, with Sanford Dole as its president. Following a brief and unsuccessful revolt of native Hawaiians to restore the power of the queen, Liliuokalani and many of her followers were tried for treason, convicted, and imprisoned. The queen's heir unsuccessfully appealed to the United States for help. President Cleveland condemned the overthrow of the monarchy and said it was, "a misuse of the name and power of the United States."

During the annexation ceremonies in 1898, Queen Liliuokalani refused to attend the event. She refused to see the Hawaiian flag lowered and the United States flag raised over her palace. Instead she spent the day in church praying, hoping somehow for a government that favored her people. Liliuokalani continued to live in Hawaii and to attend most state functions. She regained some of the royal family's land and property. In 1917, Queen Liliuokalani had a stroke and died in Honolulu. She was 79 years old.

In 1898, Hawaii was annexed by the United States, and in 1900, it became a U.S. territory. On August 21, 1959, it became the 50th American state. In 1993, Congress and President Clinton formally apologized for the overthrow of the Kingdom of Hawaii.

"Aloha a hui hou."

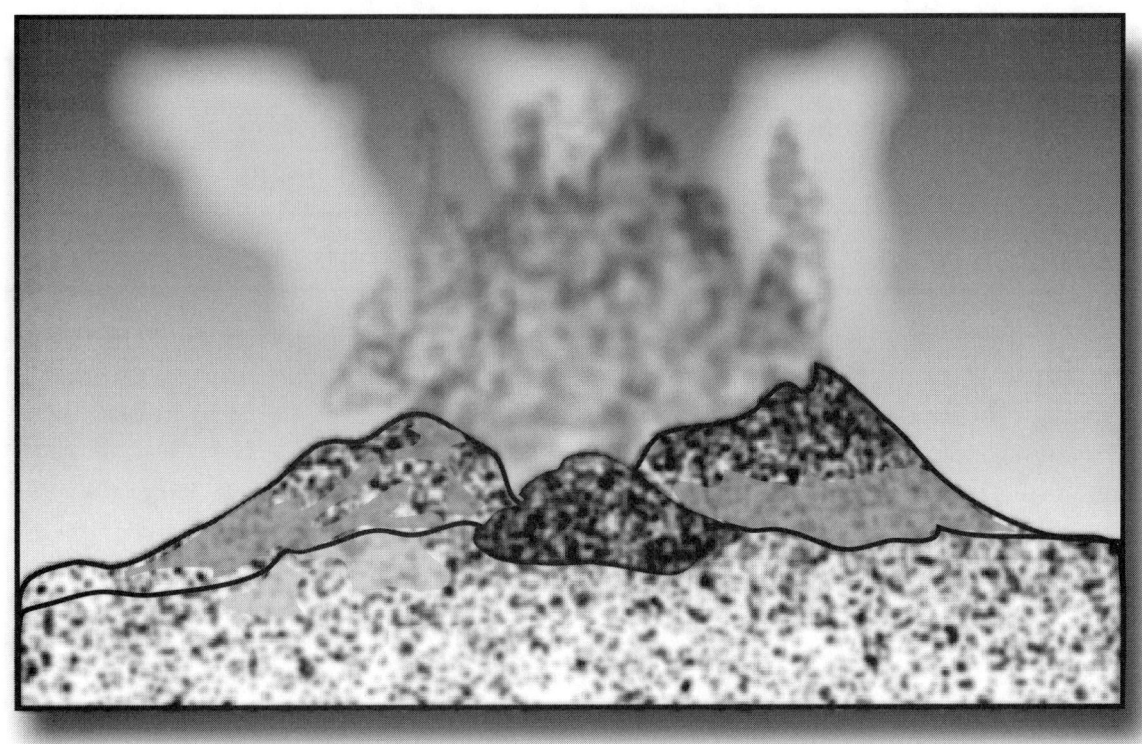

Reading Engagement: Grade 8   Level Four, Lesson 1: American Royalty, Part II

Name: _____ Date: _____

Level Four, Lesson 1: American Royalty, Part II (cont.)

Reading Guide for "American Royalty, Part II"

BEFORE READING

Before reading "American Royalty, Part II," complete the **Before Reading** section of the Reading Guide.

A. Prereading Activity: Assessing Background Knowledge

Hawaiian Royalty

Directions: How much do you remember about Hawaii and its kings and queens? Answer these questions before looking back to American Royalty, Part I.

1. Who were the first and last Hawaiian monarchs?

   _____

   _____

2. How long did the Hawaiian monarchy last?

   _____

3. What form of government replaced the monarchy in Hawaii?

   _____

   _____

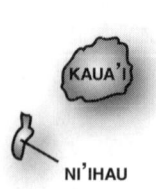
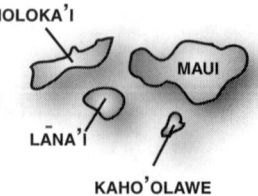
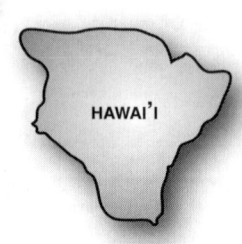

Reading Engagement: Grade 8   Level Four, Lesson 1: American Royalty, Part II

Name: _____ Date: _____

Level Four, Lesson 1: American Royalty, Part II (cont.)

B. Vocabulary: Syllables

Pronunciation Guide

Three syllabication rules will help you pronounce the names of Hawaii's kings and queens.

1. A consonant between two vowels tends to go with the second vowel unless the first vowel is accented and short.

   Examples: bro – ken, ze – bra, to – day

2. Two vowels together with separate sounds form separate syllables.

   Examples: po – li – o, ra – di – o

3. In the Hawaiian language, all vowels are distinctly pronounced.

   Example: Ka – u – a – i, O – a – hu

Directions: Divide each word into syllables, and then pronounce it correctly.

1. Liholiho   _____
2. Kaahumanu _____
3. Kamamalu   _____
4. Kamehameha _____
5. Kalakaua   _____
6. Lunalilo   _____
7. Liliuokalani _____

Level Four, Lesson 1: American Royalty, Part II (cont.)

C. Prereading Questions

1. What do you think this reading is going to be about?

   _____

   _____

2. Read the questions in the **After Reading** section of this Reading Guide.

   a. Which question do you find the most interesting?

   _____

   _____

   b. Which answer do you think will be hardest to find?

   _____

   _____

3. What is your purpose for reading this story? Finish this sentence: I am reading to find out ...

   _____

   _____

DURING READING

1. Put a check mark in the margin next to the information that answers the questions in the **After Reading** section.

2. Circle any words you don't know when you come to them in the passage.

3. Put a question mark in the margin for anything you don't understand.

Reading Engagement: Grade 8　　　　Level Four, Lesson 1: American Royalty, Part II

Name: _____ Date: _____

Level Four, Lesson 1: American Royalty, Part II (cont.)

AFTER READING

1. READING THE LINES: Answer these questions by using information in the selection.

   a. What is a *coup*?

   _____

   _____

   _____

   b. How did King Lunalilo die?

   _____

   _____

   _____

   c. Who was the last Hawaiian monarch?

   _____

   d. Who was responsible for overthrowing the monarchy of Hawaii?

   _____

   _____

   _____

   e. What does *annexation* mean?

   _____

   _____

   _____

© Mark Twain Media, Inc., Publishers

Level Four, Lesson 1: American Royalty, Part II (cont.)

2. READING BETWEEN THE LINES: Answer these questions by inferring ideas in the selection.

   a. How and when was the Hawaiian monarchy stripped of its power?

   _____
   _____
   _____
   _____

   b. What does it mean to be a "strong nationalist"? Why was Liliuokalani considered to be one?

   _____
   _____
   _____
   _____

   c. What was the participation of the United States in the coup?

   _____
   _____
   _____
   _____

   d. What adjectives were used to describe Liliuokalani?

   _____
   _____
   _____
   _____

Reading Engagement: Grade 8   Level Four, Lesson 1: American Royalty, Part II

Name: _____ Date: _____

Level Four, Lesson 1: American Royalty, Part II (cont.)

3. READING BEYOND THE LINES: Answer these questions with your own opinions.

   a. If you were Liliuokalani, would you have attended the annexation celebration? Why or why not?

   _____
   _____
   _____

   b. Do you think the President and the United States owed Hawaii an apology? Why or why not?

   _____
   _____
   _____
   _____

   c. What benefits do Hawaiians now have as a state in the United States?

   _____
   _____
   _____
   _____

ASSESSMENT/REINFORCEMENT

A. Examine the Hawaiian Language Dictionary at www.traveltraveltravel.com/haw_language.htm to unlock the Hawaiian greeting at the end of this reading:

"Aloha a hui hou."

_____

Level Four, Lesson 1: American Royalty, Part II (cont.)

B. Using the Internet and other reference sources, complete the corresponding name, nickname, color, and flower for each Hawaiian island.

	Island	Nickname	Color	Flower
1.	O'ahu	The _____ Place	Yellow	_____
2.	_____	The Friendly Island	_____	*kukui*
3.	Lāna'i	The _____ Island	Orange	_____
4.	_____	The Valley Island	_____	*lokelani*
5.	Kaua'i	The _____ Island	_____	_____
6.	_____	The Big Island	Red	_____
7.	Ni'ihau	The _____ Island	_____	*pupu,* shell
8.	_____	The Forgotten Island	_____	_____

C. Using the Internet and other reference sources, match the Hawaiian word in the first column with its corresponding English word in the second column.

1. _____ *hale*
2. _____ *kai*
3. _____ *mahalo*
4. _____ *maikai*
5. _____ *makuakane*
6. _____ *makua*
7. _____ *tutukane*
8. _____ *tutuwahine, tutu*

A. mother
B. good
C. house
D. grandfather
E. thank you
F. father
G. grandmother
H. salt water (ocean)

Level Four, Lesson 2: The United States Constitution

The United States Constitution: Beyond the Bill of Rights

constitution: The basic laws and principles under which a country, state, or organization is governed

Constitution: The written constitution of the United States of America, drafted in 1787 and ratified in 1788, creating and defining the rights and liberties of the American people

    The United States Constitution is the oldest written constitution in the world. At the core is our belief in the inalienable rights of all people, the goal toward which we strive. The phrase "We the people" at the beginning of the document puts forth our belief that the people, not the state or the federal government, are the source of power. The Constitution is the promise of democracy for all citizens.

    The purpose of the Constitution is to provide a system to enunciate basic democratic values and principles with which we can live and solve our problems. It is remarkably adaptable to new issues, new challenges, and new problems.

    Constitutional amendments are changes to the Constitution. The purpose of amendments is to adapt the Constitution to changing times and to address new issues that were not earlier considered. Since its ratification, Congressional representatives have proposed more than 10,000 amendments (such as prohibiting dueling and flag burning); 33 of these have been formalized (like equality of rights regardless of gender and non-Congressional interference in slavery) and sent to states for ratification. Despite the thousands of proposed amendments, the Constitution has only been amended 27 times since its adoption. The first 10 amendments, known as the Bill of Rights, were ratified in 1791 and were conditional for some states in ratifying the Constitution. The Bill of Rights sets forth the limitations of the federal government and outlined those things the federal government cannot do.

Voting Rights/Civil Rights. The 13th, 14th, 15th, 19th, 23rd, 24th, and 26th amendments all have to do with voting rights and/or citizens' rights. The 13th, 14th, and 15th Amendments extend democratic principles to those who were previously excluded. The 13th Amendment (1865) abolished slavery. The 15th Amendment (1870) gave the right to vote to African-American men who previously had been slaves. The 19th Amendment (1920) gave voting rights to women, and the 26th Amendment (1971) gave the right to vote to 18-year-olds. The 23rd Amendment (1961) gave Washington, D.C., citizens the right to elect representatives to the electoral college, a right previously denied them. The 24th Amendment (1964) prohibited states from denying the right to vote to anyone who failed to pay his taxes.

Level Four, Lesson 2: The United States Constitution (cont.)

The 14th Amendment (1868) has become one of the most important amendments to the Constitution. This amendment sets forth two important aspects of our democracy: due process and equal protection under the law. It says "all persons born or naturalized in the United States, and subject to the jurisdiction thereof" are citizens of the United States and of the states in which they reside. The purpose of the 14th Amendment was to recognize former slaves as citizens. It prohibits any state from depriving "any person of life, liberty, or property without due process of law" or denying anyone

"equal protection of the law." Over the years, the 14th Amendment has evolved through Supreme Court interpretation to prohibit states from denying people the same rights that the federal government cannot deny under the Bill of Rights.

Presidential Amendments: The 12th, 20th, 22nd, and 25th Amendments have to do with the presidency. The 12th Amendment (1804) addressed a specific problem that occurred during the 1800 Presidential election when Thomas Jefferson and Aaron Burr received the same number of electoral votes. Prior to the 12th Amendment, the law specified that the person with the greatest number of votes became President, and the person with the second number of votes was Vice President. The 12th Amendment specified that voters cast separate ballots for President and Vice President.

The 20th Amendment (1933) changed the inauguration date from March 4th to January 20th, thus limiting the time of a lame-duck president. The 22nd Amendment (1951) limited the president to two terms, and the 25th Amendment (1967) outlined the procedures should a president become incapacitated. It also specified that a president may appoint a new vice president if that office becomes vacant, subject to confirmation by both Houses of Congress.

Miscellaneous Amendments: The 11th Amendment (1795) prohibited citizens of one state or foreign citizens from suing another state in a federal court. The 16th Amendment (1913) gave Congress the right to pass a tax on people's income. The 17th (1913) changed the way U.S. senators are elected. Instead of election by the state legislature, the Amendment gave people the right to elect their senators. The 18th Amendment (1919) prohibited the sale, manufacture, or importation of intoxicating liquors in the United States. The 21st Amendment (1933) repealed the 18th Amendment (the only amendment to be repealed!). The 27th Amendment (1992) was written in 1789 as part of the first 12 amendments proposed and was finally ratified in 1992. The Amendment requires that compensation for senators and representatives cannot be increased until another election has passed.

Twenty-seven amendments in little more than 200 years is a remarkable testament to our nation's commitment to the dignity and worth of every person. The Constitution is a "living" document adaptable to new issues, new challenges, and new problems, yet it still protects the rights of 288,000,000 Americans in their beliefs, thoughts, and emotions.

Reading Engagement: Grade 8 · Level Four, Lesson 2: The United States Constitution

Level Four, Lesson 2: The United States Constitution (cont.)

Reading Guide for "The United States Constitution"

BEFORE READING

Before reading "The United States Constitution," complete the **Before Reading** section of the Reading Guide.

A. Prereading Activity: Assessing Background Knowledge

The United States Constitution Cloze Paragraph

Directions: What do you know about the Constitution? Read the preamble to the Constitution, filling in the blank lines with what you think goes there.*

We the _____ of the United States,

in order to form a more perfect _____,

establish _____, insure domestic _____,

provide for the common _____, promote the

general _____, and secure the _____

of _____ to ourselves and our _____,

do ordain and establish this _____ for the

United States of _____.

*If you don't know, go to www.house.gov/Constitution/Constitution.html or find a copy of the Constitution in a reference book.

Level Four, Lesson 2: The United States Constitution (cont.)

B. Vocabulary: Understanding Jargon

Social Studies Terms

Directions: Use the glossary of your social studies text or other reference sources to define these social studies (government) terms.

1. electoral college _____
   _____
   _____

2. inalienable rights _____
   _____
   _____

3. democratic values _____
   _____
   _____

4. Constitutional amendment _____
   _____
   _____

5. due process _____
   _____
   _____

6. equal protection under the law _____
   _____
   _____

Reading Engagement: Grade 8 — Level Four, Lesson 2: The United States Constitution

Name: _____ Date: _____

Level Four, Lesson 2: The United States Constitution (cont.)

7. lame-duck president _____
   _____
   _____

C. Prereading Questions

1. What do you think this reading is going to be about?
   _____
   _____

2. Read the questions in the **After Reading** section of this Reading Guide.

   a. Which question do you find the most interesting?
      _____
      _____

   b. Which answer do you think will be hardest to find?
      _____
      _____

3. What is your purpose for reading this story? Finish this sentence: I am reading to find out ...
   _____
   _____

DURING READING

1. Put a check mark in the margin next to the information that answers the questions in the **After Reading** section.

2. Circle any words you don't know when you come to them in the passage.

3. Put a question mark in the margin for anything you don't understand.

Reading Engagement: Grade 8   Level Four, Lesson 2: The United States Constitution
Name: _____   Date: _____

Level Four, Lesson 2: The United States Constitution (cont.)

AFTER READING

1. READING THE LINES: Answer these questions by using information in the selection.

    a. How does the U.S. Constitution begin? Why is this significant?

    _____

    _____

    _____

    b. How many Constitutional amendments have been ratified?

    _____

    c. Which amendment abolished slavery?

    _____

    d. Which is the only amendment that has been repealed?

    _____

2. READING BETWEEN THE LINES: Answer these questions by inferring ideas in the selection.

    a. Besides states or countries, what other groups or organizations might have a constitution?

    _____

    _____

    b. What does it mean when it is said that the Constitution is a "living" document?

    _____

    _____

    _____

Level Four, Lesson 2: The United States Constitution (cont.)

c. To what does the pronoun "these" refer in paragraph 3, sentence 3?

d. What is the topic sentence for this reading?

3. READING BEYOND THE LINES: Answer these questions with your own opinions.

   a. In your opinion, what is the most important amendment among those discussed in the reading? Why?

   b. What are some things our government can't do to us?

   c. Do you think 18-year-olds are mature enough to vote? Why or why not?

Level Four, Lesson 2: The United States Constitution (cont.)

ASSESSMENT/REINFORCEMENT

A. Directions: Take this post-test and see what you learned about the Constitution and its amendments from this reading.

Which amendment makes the change? Write its number on the blank next to the statement.

_____ 1. This amendment abolished slavery.

_____ 2. This amendment allowed 18-year-olds the right to vote.

_____ 3. This amendment allowed women to vote.

_____ 4. This amendment prohibits compensation for senators or representatives from going into effect before the next election.

_____ 5. This amendment specified that voters cast separate ballots for President and Vice President.

_____ 6. This amendment prohibits states from denying people the same rights that the federal government cannot deny.

_____ 7. This amendment gives citizens of Washington, D.C., the right to elect representatives to the electoral college.

_____ 8. This amendment changes the date of the president's inauguration.

_____ 9. This amendment gave Congress the right to collect taxes on people's income.

_____ 10. This amendment prohibited the sale and manufacturing of alcohol.

_____ 11. This amendment repealed the prohibition on alcohol.

_____ 12. This amendment gave the right to vote to African-Americans who were former slaves.

_____ 13. This amendment prohibits a president from serving more than two terms.

Reading Engagement: Grade 8   Level Four, Lesson 2: The United States Constitution

Name: _____   Date: _____

Level Four, Lesson 2: The United States Constitution (cont.)

B. Next to the number of each amendment, try to write in as few words as possible the purpose of the amendment. The amendments have been grouped into categories to help you.

Voting Rights/Civil Rights

13th _____
14th _____
15th _____
19th _____
23rd _____
24th _____
26th _____

Presidential Amendments

12th _____
20th _____
22nd _____
25th _____

Miscellaneous Amendments

11th _____
16th _____
17th _____
18th _____
21st _____
27th _____

© Mark Twain Media, Inc., Publishers

Level Four, Lesson 3: Presidential Scandals

Presidential Scandals

Whitewater, Paula Jones, and Monica Lewinsky are all scandals that occurred during the Bill Clinton administration. While they might be the most well-known today, they are far from being the only or the worst presidential scandals. Have you ever heard of Crédit Mobilier or the Whiskey Ring? These were both political and business scandals of the Grant administration. There was the Teapot Dome scandal during the Harding administration, Watergate during Nixon's administration, and the Iran-Contra scandal of the Reagan administration. Scandals happen when people are greedy or abuse power, both of which were at the heart of the presidential scandals of Ulysses S. Grant and Warren G. Harding.

Ulysses S. Grant – Crédit Mobilier of America (1867)

The Crédit Mobilier scandal is an example of the depth of political and corporate corruption during the administration of President Grant. Crédit Mobilier was a dummy construction company of the Union Pacific Railroad. It was set up by the stockholders of the Union Pacific Railroad during the building of the first transcontinental railroad. It was organized in 1864 by Oakes Ames and Thomas Durant, who drew up contracts on behalf of the railroad with themselves. They awarded construction contracts to their own company for completing the transcontinental railroad. The stockholders (including Ames and Durant) then reaped incredible profits by inflating construction costs. The actual cost of building the transcontinental railroad was about $44 million; the Crédit Mobilier charged the government more than $84 million. The corrupt stockholders made a staggering 500% profit in 1867–68.

Ulysses S. Grant

Word spread about the connection between the railroad and its construction company, especially in the press. Congress began to investigate the rumors they had been hearing about Crédit Mobilier. To block the investigation, Oakes Ames, who was also a representative from Massachusetts, bribed twenty members of Congress by offering Crédit Mobilier stock cheaply. Future President, James A. Garfield; Speaker of the House, James G. Blaine; President Grant's Vice President, Schuyler Colfax; Senator James W. Patterson of New Hampshire; Senator Henry Wilson of Massachusetts; and Representative James Brooks of New York were some of the political figures that were accused of accepting the bribes. A full investigation of the scandal was never made, but Congress did censure Ames and Brooks; there were, however, no prosecutions.

Level Four, Lesson 3: Presidential Scandals (cont.)

Grant – The Whiskey Ring (1875)

After the Civil War, whiskey taxes were raised sky-high, sometimes eight times the price of the whiskey itself. The Whiskey Ring was a group of distillers and public officials who conspired to defraud the federal government of liquor taxes. Large distillers, mainly in St. Louis, Milwaukee, and Chicago, bribed government officials in order to keep the tax proceeds for themselves. The distillers bribed the tax collectors, and the tax collectors bribed the government officials.

The Whiskey Ring was a widespread scandal that affected many people, including some who were in high government positions. A secret investigation by the U.S. Treasury Department resulted in the arrest of 238 people. Only 110 of them were convicted. President Grant's secretary, Orville E. Babcock, was acquitted through the personal intervention of the president. Many believed the Whiskey Ring was part of a plot to finance the Republican Party.

Warren G. Harding – The Teapot Dome Scandal (1921)

Warren G. Harding is often described as the worst president our country has ever had. At the very least, his presidency is remembered as one of the most corrupt to occupy the White House. Certainly it was the most corrupt administration since the Grant presidency. The Teapot Dome Scandal was a case of bribery that involved the secret leasing of naval oil reserves to private companies.

In 1912, President William Howard Taft set aside 70,000 acres of oil land in the Elk Hills of California as the Navy Oil Reserves. In 1914, President Woodrow Wilson added 10,000 acres at Teapot Dome, Wyoming. (Teapot Dome got its name from a rock formation that resembled a teapot.) These oil reserves were to be maintained by the government until the navy needed to "use, store, exchange, or sell" the oil for the benefit of the United States.

In 1921, President Harding was persuaded by his secretary of the interior, Albert Fall, to issue a secret executive order transferring control of the naval oil reserves from the Department of the Navy to the Department of the Interior. Albert Fall, then secretary of the interior,

Warren G. Harding

Level Four, Lesson 3: Presidential Scandals (cont.)

had control of the reserves. In 1922, Fall leased the land to two powerful oil operators, Harry F. Sinclair of Mammoth Oil Company and Edward L. Doheny of Pan American Petroleum Company, in exchange for cash and gifts. Fall persuaded the president that the oil was leaking onto private sites, and Doheny and Sinclair would drill before all the oil leaked away, saving it for the government. Fall received almost $400,000 for allowing these two oil companies to drill on public lands and to sell the oil for private profit.

Secrets are not kept long in Washington, D.C. The scandal soon came to light with Congressional demands that the leases be abrogated. A Congressional committee, headed by Senator Thomas J. Walsh of Montana, was formed to investigate the affair. The investigations led to criminal prosecutions. President Harding himself was not involved in the scandal and was just beginning to learn of the problems when he died. His death left the fallout from the scandal to his successor, Calvin Coolidge. President Coolidge handled the problem skillfully and was able to avoid damaging his own administration.

Secretary of the Navy Edwin Denby was cleared of all charges in the investigation but was forced to resign from Coolidge's Cabinet. Albert Fall resigned from the Cabinet after undergoing criminal prosecution; he was sentenced to a year in prison and fined $100,000 for accepting bribes. He was the first presidential Cabinet member to go to prison for his actions while in office. Doheny and Sinclair were both fined $100,000. Doheny served a few months in prison and later died under suspicious conditions; Sinclair was imprisoned for a short time for contempt of Congress and jury tampering. All three were acquitted of conspiracy to defraud the government.

In December of 1927, the United States Supreme Court invalidated the leases to Doheny and Sinclair, noting they had been obtained by fraud and corruption. "Teapot Dome" has been added to American political vernacular as a synonym for public corruption.

Albert Fall and Edward Doheny were both fined and sent to prison for their part in the Teapot Dome Scandal.

Reading Engagement: Grade 8 Level Four, Lesson 3: Presidential Scandals

Name: _____ Date: _____

Level Four, Lesson 3: Presidential Scandals (cont.)

Reading Guide for "Presidential Scandals"

BEFORE READING

Before reading "Presidential Scandals," complete the **Before Reading** section of the Reading Guide.

A. Prereading Activity: Activating Background Knowledge.

What Do …

1. Presidents Bill Clinton, Richard Nixon, and Ronald Reagan have in common?

   _____
   _____
   _____

2. Whitewater, Paula Jones, and Monica Lewinsky have in common?

   _____
   _____
   _____

3. Crédit Mobilier, the Whiskey Ring, the Teapot Dome, and Watergate have in common?

   _____
   _____
   _____
   _____

Richard M. Nixon

Reading Engagement: Grade 8

Level Four, Lesson 3: Presidential Scandals

Name: _____ Date: _____

Level Four, Lesson 3: Presidential Scandals (cont.)

B. Vocabulary: Parts of Speech and Word Meanings

Action Words

Directions: An action verb makes a sentence move, physically or mentally. Six of the words in the Word Bank are action verbs. Choose which six are action verbs, and then use each of them in a sentence on the lines below.

```
WORD BANK
   dummy      inflate      censure      defraud
   acquit     lease        abrogate     distiller
```

1. _____

2. _____

3. _____

4. _____

5. _____

6. _____

C. Prereading Questions

1. What do you think this reading is going to be about?

_____

_____

© Mark Twain Media, Inc., Publishers

Level Four, Lesson 3: Presidential Scandals (cont.)

2. Read the questions in the **After Reading** section of this Reading Guide.

   a. Which question do you find the most interesting?

   _____

   _____

   b. Which answer do you think will be hardest to find?

   _____

   _____

3. What is your purpose for reading this story? Finish this sentence: I am reading to find out …

   _____

   _____

DURING READING

1. Put a check mark in the margin next to the information that answers the questions in the **After Reading** section.

2. Circle any words you don't know when you come to them in the passage.

3. Put a question mark in the margin for anything you don't understand.

AFTER READING

1. READING THE LINES: Answer these questions by using information in the selection.

   a. What is a political scandal?

   _____

   _____

Reading Engagement: Grade 8   Level Four, Lesson 3: Presidential Scandals

Name: _____ Date: _____

Level Four, Lesson 3: Presidential Scandals (cont.)

    b.   Why do political scandals happen?

_____

_____

_____

    c.   What was the Crédit Mobilier?

_____

_____

_____

    d.   What was the profit for corrupt stockholders?

_____

    e.   What are naval oil reserves?

_____

_____

_____

2.   READING BETWEEN THE LINES: Answer these questions by inferring ideas in the selection.

    a.   What was the transcontinental railroad?

_____

_____

_____

© Mark Twain Media, Inc., Publishers

Level Four, Lesson 3: Presidential Scandals (cont.)

    b.   What does it mean to "inflate construction costs"?

    _____
    _____
    _____

    c.   Do you think the punishment for Ames and Brooks was fair? Why or why not?

    _____
    _____
    _____
    _____

    d.   Why were the government taxes on whiskey so high following the Civil War?

    _____
    _____
    _____
    _____

3.   READING BEYOND THE LINES: Answer these questions with your own opinions.

    a.   Do you think Albert Fall's punishment fit his crimes? Why or why not?

    _____
    _____
    _____

    b.   Of all the scandals described in this reading, which do you think was the worst? Why?

    _____
    _____
    _____
    _____

Level Four, Lesson 3: Presidential Scandals (cont.)

ASSESSMENT/REINFORCEMENT

A. Do a little research on the scandals that were not described in the reading: Watergate, Iran-Contra, and Whitewater. Prepare a handout for your classmates on these presidential scandals.

B. Fill in the blanks in each clue below, and then find and circle the word in the word search puzzle. Words may be printed forward, backward, horizontally, vertically, or diagonally.

1. Taxes on this item were eight times higher than the price of the product itself. _____
2. A naval oil reserve in Wyoming _____ _____
3. Dummy construction company for the Union Pacific Railroad _____ _____
4. Secretary of the Interior who allowed private oil companies to drill on public lands _____ _____
5. Representative who was one of the organizers of the Crédit Mobilier company _____ _____
6. Whiskey distillers attempted to _____ the federal government of liquor taxes.
7. The Crédit Mobilier and Whiskey Ring scandals happened during this president's administration. _____ _____
8. The Teapot Dome scandal was part of the corruption surrounding the _____ _____ _____ administration.
9. Money or gifts given to induce someone to do something wrong or illegal _____
10. An act that offends or shocks the moral feelings of the community and leads to disgrace _____

```
Q T N T G W P L Q U Q T V T U
G W N E M O D T O P A E T Q R
Q N C A D U A R F E D L G S E
A M I H R M A D O M R J B E I
L K M D F G R K G F X R Q P L
O A J P R E S C H K I H I S I
X F D C Q A K S I B I C E L B
O R Z N Q H H A E E Q M J Z O
Z Y U C A R Q G F S A B K G M
G E Z G E C Y R N S S C T Q T
S K L G S D S D E E R Y N Q I
R S Z K C S A K H B R Y L N D
G I Z G R V A S L Q Z R Z U E
D H M J S O Q S A F A R A R R
B W A L B E R T F A L L A W C
```